THE YIN AND YANG OF LEADERSHIP

A theoretical and practical guide to democratic leading

Intentional leadership

Appreciative leadership

François Héon, M.A.Sc., Ph.D.

Author: François Héon, M.A.Sc., Ph.D.

www.francoisheon.com

Published by François Héon

Editing & design: Carole Zabbal-Wynne (www.carolezabbal.com)

Design: Chantal Fleurent (cfbureautech.com)

For permission requests please email:
E. fheon@francoisheon.com | www.francoisheon.com

ISBN: 9780993955372 | First Edition

François Héon

Keywords: leadership, leadership development, individual leadership, collective leadership, appreciative leadership, intentional leadership, integrative leadership

A Consulting Anecdote
from the Field

It's 1994. I'm working on a democracy development project in Burundi, Africa, and riding in a huge military transport truck driven by a Burundian soldier. The truck we're in is called (in French) a '*Je m'en fous,*' which you could translate into English as 'I couldn't care less' or 'I don't give a f***.'

The Burundians call these huge military trucks "I couldn't care less" because when they drive down the road, they don't care if you're in their way. They really don't. Whether you're riding up a hill on a bicycle piled with empty glass bottles, or walking with a child on your back and 60 pounds of wood on your head, a '*Je m'en fous*' will drive you straight into the ditch if you don't move out. A '*Je m'en fous*' dominates the road, period.

As we're driving, I see how the soldier confirms this Burundian reputation of the '*Je m'en fous*' dominating the road, and I ask him: "Do you really have to drive this way?" And the soldier answers: "Yes, absolutely! If I don't drive a '*Je m'en fous*' this way, people will not respect me."

TABLE OF CONTENTS

INTRODUCTION

A 25-YEAR JOURNEY DEVELOPING A NEW INTEGRATIVE LEADERSHIP MODEL

T his book can be described as the conclusion of a 25-year life inquiry I began in 1991 as a Ph.D. student in organizational behavior at Case Western Reserve University in Cleveland, Ohio (see Figure 1). After completing two years of the Ph.D. coursework, filled with the abundance of learning, I felt the need to interrupt my academic studies and pursue different consulting experiences before producing an original dissertation.

After working in the fields of democracy development in Africa (1994-1996), mental health community services in Montreal, Canada (1997-2000), and more clinical training in both group and individual psychotherapy, I eventually returned to my original passion of leadership consulting in 2000. In 2002, I joined the international human resources group of Adecco, a staffing firm based in Zurich, Switzerland. I led the development of their new consulting endeavor, The House of Leaders, in Canada.

It's at that time that I introduced the Significant Leader Exercise, which I've been using ever since as the basic introductory exercise to all my leadership workshops. And as you will discover, it has become a central exercise to this book. I hope it will prove useful to you in your own leadership development.

Figure 1: Overall inquiry process that led to this book

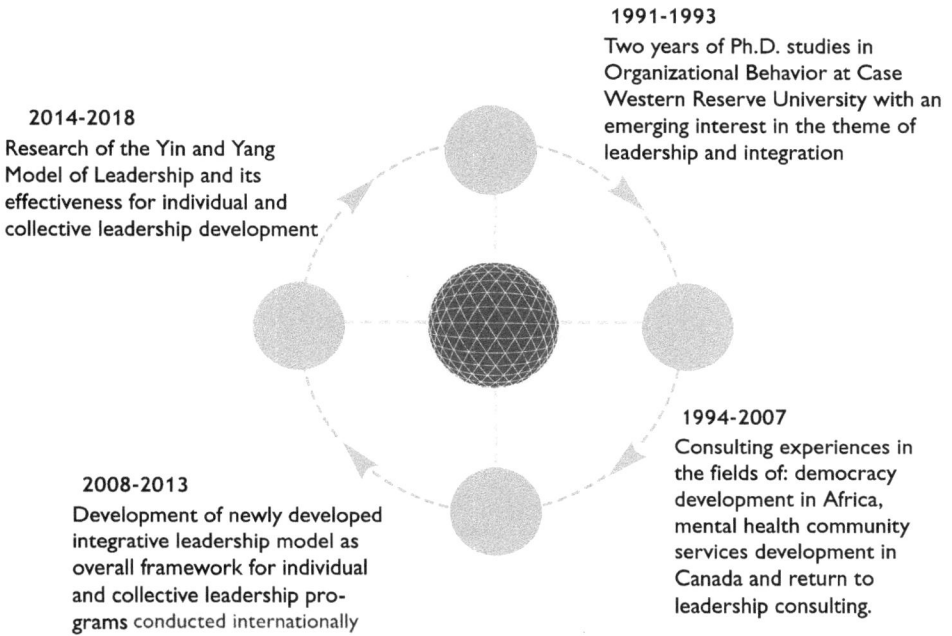

1991-1993
Two years of Ph.D. studies in Organizational Behavior at Case Western Reserve University with an emerging interest in the theme of leadership and integration

2014-2018
Research of the Yin and Yang Model of Leadership and its effectiveness for individual and collective leadership development

1994-2007
Consulting experiences in the fields of: democracy development in Africa, mental health community services development in Canada and return to leadership consulting.

2008-2013
Development of newly developed integrative leadership model as overall framework for individual and collective leadership pro-grams conducted internationally

The Significant Leader Exercise: Finding Two Leadership Factors

When I designed my first leadership workshops for managers, I decided to build my opening presentation on leadership in a participative way and highlight good leadership through the participants' own best examples of good leadership.

I call this exercise the **Significant Leader Exercise**. I start by asking each participant to identify *the* one person they have known throughout their life who stands out as his or her best example of leadership (e.g., a parent, a coach, a teacher, a friend, a former or current manager). Then, I ask each participant to identify the singular, most prominent characteristic or quality that distinguished this leadership exemplar from every other person they've ever known.

In the participant's eyes, what characteristic made that person such an outstanding example of good leadership? Try this exercise yourself!

Try This!

Who is your best example of leadership?

What quality or characteristic do you find distinguishes that person's leadership the most?

Workshop after workshop, I collected the significant characteristics of good leadership that the participants were listing as their prime example of leadership on flipcharts. And I noticed every time how each set generally fell into either of two categories.

On one hand, participants highlighted qualities like their leader's vision, determination, courage, initiative, decisiveness, and task- and results-focus. On the other hand, they also underlined their leader's caring, listening, respect, empathy, openness, coaching, and uniting as the other complementary set of characteristics.

Recognizing a bidimensional representation of leadership wasn't such a surprise. It has emerged as a dominant framework of leadership theory in the last 70 years, following *Initiating Structure* and *Consideration* as the first two behavioral leadership factors. These were followed by their generic equivalent, *task/result* and *relationship/person* orientations. What was more surprising was to discover the *variety* of terms that could be used to describe each of these bidimensional factors in behavioral theories as well as in more contemporary process-oriented and learning theories of leadership, in psychology, and in ancient philosophies as well.

Not only did these theories and philosophies speak of the act of leading as combining two factors, they also consistently revealed that these two factors were actually interrelated and constitutive of the unifying process we call leadership.

I've since developed a leadership model based on this recurring pattern with *intentionality* and *appreciation* as complementary factors, and I've been successfully using this model in leadership workshops with thousands of leaders and groups from around the world. Clients have also shared how easy it was for them to apply the model on their own with much success. It's therefore a model that not only synthesizes previous theories, it's also one that can be easily passed on and reapplied in different settings and by different people – i.e., it's versatile!

In summary, this book develops and offers the Yin and Yang Model of Leadership as:

- An accessible leadership model for any individual and collective wishing to develop their own leadership.

- A bidimensional model that integrates the pattern of complementary leadership factors found throughout leadership theory, psychology, and ancient philosophies (see more in Part I).

- A model that addresses the different levels of interpretation of leadership, including that of functional leadership as the capacity to lead a task and existential leadership, or self-leadership, as the capacity to lead one's own existence.

Part I presents an extensive literature review that highlights how bidimensional and integrative representations of leadership have been consistently presented in leadership theory, psychology, and eastern philosophies such as Taoism and Yogic philosophy in the last 3,000 years. The theoretical review sets the theoretical basis for the following presentation of the Yin and Yang Leadership Model and validates *intentionality* and *appreciation* as its two complementary leadership factors.

Following the literature review, Part II explores more concretely how any individual can lead intentionally and appreciatively with this new integrative leadership model. A brief discussion also concludes of Part II.

Part III explores how collectives can use the same model and develop their own collective leadership, whether they be a pair of individuals or a group of any size.

A note on three subsections to facilitate your reading in Parts II and III

Consulting Anecdotes from the Field

Anecdotes from my consulting experience in organizational development are interspersed throughout the book to help highlight various aspects of leadership and the application of both appreciative and intentional principles in real life.

Words of Wisdom

Quotes of wisdom are also spread throughout the book to complement important leadership themes.

Try This!

These sections highlight examples or propose exercises that are easy to apply and can significantly enhance your own individual and collective leadership.

A Note on References to Mary P. Follett's ideas

You'll notice frequent references to the management pioneer Mary Parker Follett throughout the book, and especially in Part III, which deals with collective leadership.

Follett's processual philosophy and vision of leadership as an integrative process serves as the foundational management philosophy for the Yin and Yang Model and underlies many of the ideas I propose in this book. There has been a historical lack of recognition of her work which has encouraged me to be even more generous in sharing many examples of her prophetic writings.

A Note on 'Collective Leadership'

The notion of collective leadership used in this book is operationally defined as a set of cooperatively-oriented cognitions, attitudes, and actions through which team members convert member inputs to team outputs.

The word collective includes a pair of individuals as well as groups of three or more.

PART I

REVIEW OF BIDIMENSIONAL AND INTEGRATIVE REPRESENTATIONS OF LEADERSHIP IN MANAGEMENT, PSYCHOLOGY, AND PHILOSOPHY

This chapter presents an extensive review of the literature on the recurring bidimensional and integrative representations of leadership in management theory, psychology, and eastern philosophies such as Taoism and Yogic philosophy.

Bidimensional and integrative
representations of leadership
in management

Four leadership eras highlighted by organizational theorist Richard L. Daft (2008) will provide a chronology to structure this review of bidimensional theories of leadership in management literature.

1. Great Person leadership
2. Rational management
3. Team (or lateral) leadership
4. Learning leadership

   - The Leadership Experience (2008)

1. The Great Person Theory

This first specific theory of leaders emerged in the late 19th century and was originally termed the 'Great Man Theory' and more recently renamed for gender neutrality as the 'Great Person Theory.' Thomas Carlisle's book *On Heroes, Hero-Worship, and the Heroic in History* (1840), a classic reference on the subject, refers to leaders as born heroes, whether they be a leading prophet, poet, or king. Carlisle presented leadership as a question of heredity or destiny, and the possibility of developing leadership or becoming a leader wasn't a consideration at the time.

While the Great Man or Great Person Theory praised the exclusive attributes and powers of those who could command power over others, these same notions of command and power-over became increasingly dissonant with modern, early 20th-century democratic ideas of equality, freedom and self-government.

Ordway Tead (1935), an American organizational scholar of the early 20th century, emphasized how the notion of 'leader' was being redefined in a new democratic world and increasingly in contrast with the conventional notion of authoritarian leader as commander over others, as presented in the Great Man Theory.

Tead (1935) writes in *The Art of Leadership*:

> On every hand today the cry is for more and better leaders. Command is interested in getting some associated action which the commander wants to secure. It is an exercise of power over people. Leadership is interested in how people can be brought to work together for a common end effectively and happily. It implies, as it has been said, the use and creation of power with people.

2. Rational management

To transcend the hero-worshipping posture of the Great Man Theory, trait theorists such as Tead and others (e.g., Bowden, 1926; Gibb, 1947; Stogdill, 1948) tried to list distinctive qualities that leaders exhibit to better understand their distinguishing influences. These qualities have remained consistent over time and have been eventually classified into two groupings of traits:

1) Task-oriented traits; and

2) Relationship-oriented traits.

Two Leadership Behavioral Groupings: Leading by Consideration and Initiating Structure

Considering the situational limits of trait theory, since not every trait is appropriate for every situation, Ohio State University researchers sought to find the smallest number of dimensions that would adequately describe leader behavior as perceived by the leader's subordinates and the leaders themselves. The results from both subordinate and leader reports was the isolation of two identical factors, which they termed *initiating structure* and *consideration.*

Table 1: Original definitions – Initiating structure and consideration

INITIATING **STRUCTURE**

A task-oriented leadership style, initiating structure is the degree to which a leader defines and organizes his role and the roles of followers, is oriented toward goal-attainment, and establishes well-defined patterns and channels of communication.

CONSIDERATION

Consideration is the extent to which a leader exhibits concern for the welfare of the members of the group. This factor is oriented towards interpersonal relationships, mutual trust, and friendship.

This leadership style is people-oriented.

Table 2: Subscales of initiating structure and consideration

INITIATING STRUCTURE SUBSCALES

REPRESENTATIONS
Speaks and acts as the representative of the group (5 items).

PERSUASIVENESS
Uses persuasion and argument
effectively; exhibits strong
convictions (10 items).

INITIATION OF STRUCTURE
Clearly defines own role, and lets
followers know what is expected
(10 items).

ROLE ASSUMPTION
Actively exercises the leadership
role rather that surrendering
leadership to others (10 items).

PRODUCTION EMPHASIS
Applies pressure for productive
output (10 items).

PREDICTIVE ACCURACY
Exhibits foresight and ability to
predict outcome accurately (5 items).

SUPERIOR PRINCIPLE
Maintains cordial relations with
superiors; has influence with them;
is striving for higher status (10 items).

CONSIDERATION SUBSCALES

DEMAND RECONCILIATION
Reconciles conflicting demands and
reduces disorder to system (5 items).

TOLERANCE OF UNCERTAINTY
Is able to tolerate uncertainty and
postponement without anxiety or
upset (10 items).

TOLERANCE AND FREEDOM
Allows followers scope for initiative,
decision and action (10 items).

CONSIDERATION
Regards the comfort, well-being,
status, and contributions of
followers (10 items).

INTEGRATION
Maintains a closely-knit
organization; resolves inter-
member conflicts (5 items).

Following Ohio State's pioneering studies, researchers at the University of Michigan replicated Ohio State's findings and proposed two alternative leadership concepts, which they termed *job-centered* and *employee-centered* leadership. Blake and Mouton from the University of Texas also proposed a new behavioral model called the Leadership Grid, and proposed *concern for production* and *concern for people* as the two main leadership factors (1964). And in a similar fashion, Fiedler's contingency model (1967) and, later, Hersey and Blanchard's Situational Leadership Theory (1969) defined two behavioral factors of leadership as *task behavior* (guidance) on the one hand and *relationship behavior* (supportive behavior) on the other.

You can see a summary of these pairs of behavioral factors in Table 3.

Table 3: The two principles of leader behavior

	TASK-ORIENTED PRINCIPLE	PEOPLE-ORIENTED PRINCIPLE
1957 Ohio State University studies	Initiating Structure	Consideration
1964 Blake and Mouton's Leadership Grid University of Texas	Concern for production	Concern for people
1966 University of Michigan studies	Job-centered	Employee-centered
1969 Hersey andBlanchard's Situational Leadership	Task behavior (guidance)	Relationship behavior (Supportive Behavior)

3. Team, or Lateral, Leadership

In an increasingly changing and uncertain environment in the 1970s, 'teamwork' and 'personal influence' became more and more relevant to the understanding of leadership. Characteristic of this period was the development of power and influence theories such as *transformational leadership,* based on James MacGregor Burns' (1978) work that emphasized a person's personal power to inspire other people to work beyond expectations for a common goal.

Bass and Avolio (1997) followed and developed *transformational theory* and brought into focus two important dimensions of leadership: that leadership was *relational* and that *the motivations of leaders and followers* were key to understanding leadership and change.

Burns' work introduced a process perspective (i.e. dynamically interrelated) and challenged researchers to abandon the leader-focused model and to take up the study of leadership aimed at "realizing goals mutually held by both leaders and followers," thus seeing leadership as a process of mutual engagement between people more than a question of possessing particular individual attributes to wield more power over others.

Burns adds:

> To perceive the working of leadership in social causation as motivational and volitional rather than simply as 'economic' or 'ideological' or 'institutional' is to perceive not a linear sequence of stimulus response 'sets' or 'stages' not even a network of sequential and cross-cutting forces, but a rich and pulsating stream of leadership-followership forces flowing through the whole social process.

The Need for Process

Although Ohio State's two-leader behavioral factors are some of the best examples of longstanding factors manifested throughout leadership theories, Quinn, Spreitzer, and Hart (1992), and others (Weissenberg & Kavanach, 2006) challenged the static bipolar categorization of managerial leadership and proposed the need for process and the notion of interpenetration, a dynamic integration of both polarities.

While *Consideration* and *Initiating Structure* in Hemphill and Coons' (1957) *Leader Behavior Description Questionnaire* (LBDQ) were generally assumed to be uncorrelated and independent factors, a review of 13 studies with the LBDQ showed a significant relationship between *task* and *people* concerns. This relationship between task and relationship orientations has been overlooked, with the exception of Blake and Mouton's notion of high-high leaders, meaning that good leaders should be both highly focused on task orientation and also highly focused on relationship orientation. This is consistent with longstanding criticism of trait theories that limit their focus to particular leadership qualities, but not so much on the actual activity or process that these qualities express.

4. Learning Theories: Leading with Two Learning Attitudes

> The greatest discovery of my generation is that human beings can change their life by changing their attitude.
>
> — William James (1890)

Learning theorists changed their focus from the leader's behaviors to the leader's attitudes. Attitudes that precede and orient behaviors, and, as William James famously proposed earlier, attitudes that can help a person adapt and transform their own constantly changing life.

Two Learning Orientations of Self-Directed Learning: Leading by *Retrolearning* and *Protolearning*

Organizational scholars David Kolb (1988) and, later, Boyatzis and Kolb (1991) developed the notion of *self-directed learning* which combines two complementary learning orientations they term, 1) *protolearning* and 2) *retrolearning*. More recently, Goleman, Boyatzis and McKee posited in *Primal Leadership* (2002) that "the crux of leadership is self-directed learning."

Kolb defined protolearning as "the formulation of scenarios, hypotheses, beliefs, and intentions, which anticipate the future" and retrolearning as "the re-examination and debriefing of past experiences, establishing general operating principles, adding cumulative quality to organizational efforts and a sense of historical continuity."

Two Principles in Systems Thinking: Leading by Emergence and Design

Learning orientations have also been transposed to groups and systems research with an outlook on leadership and organizational life as living and dynamic. According to these systems researchers, there are two different ways in which the patterns of organizations embody themselves in physical structures.

Capra and Flatau (1996) call these two complementary orientations of leadership:

1) **Embodiment through design**

and

2) **Embodiment through emergence**

They write: "We see that emergence and design can be distinguished, but can never be separated."

Complex and adaptable organizations are thus able to maintain a creative tension between emergence and design—that is, flexible, adaptive, and open to novelty (i.e. emergence), while at the same time effectively organizing their relationships to produce and market goods and services (i.e. design).

Thus, by balancing the requirements of both emergent and designed structures, these complex human organizations maximize their creativity and flourish.

Two Principles in Level 5 Leadership: Leading with Deep Personal Humility and Intense Professional Will

Leadership author and researcher Jim Collins also completed a research project studying the characteristics of Fortune 500 companies who succeeded at maintaining a level of leadership excellence and lasting prosperity in their field. His sample of "Leader Organizations" had to fulfill these criteria:

- Be a Fortune 500 company since 1965

- Demonstrate generated revenue per share three times higher than the market for over 15 years.

From a sample of 1,435 companies, Collins and his research team identified 11 organizations that maintained such levels of excellence. And like previously-mentioned leadership theories, Collins also expressed leadership excellence in a bidimensional way, which he termed **Level 5 Leadership**.

Collins states:

> These 11 companies had a 'Level 5' leader at the helm. Level 5 leaders blend the paradoxical combination of *deep personal humility with intense professional will.* This rare combination makes us question our preconceptions of what characterizes a great leader.

Level 5 leaders show humility in their capacity to appreciate people who surround them. These same leaders also have the humility to serve the long-term success of the organization or project beyond their own time at helm.

Collins adds:

> The great irony is that the animus and personal ambition that often drives people to become a Level 4 leader stands at odds with the humility required to rise to level 5.

Collins refers to the yin and yang concepts of Chinese Taoism to describe the two principles of sustained leadership excellence with the yang-like characteristics of *intense professional will,* on one hand and the yin-like characteristics of *deep personal humility* on the other (see Figure 2). As an example, Collins recognizes Abraham Lincoln as a model of this principled leadership.

Collins writes:

> It might be a stretch to compare the 11 Level 5 CEOs in our research to Lincoln, but they did display the same kind of duality.

While leadership theorists Hersey and Blanchard called for leaders to be highly task-focused and highly people-focused at the same time, Jim Collins and Gerry Porras propose a similar idea 30 years later:

> A highly visionary company doesn't want to blend yin and yang into a gray, indistinguishable circle that is neither highly yin nor highly yang; it aims to be distinctly yin and distinctly yang- both at the same time, all the time. Irrational? Perhaps. Rare? Yes. Difficult? Absolutely.

Figure 2: Jim Collin's Yin and Yang
sustained leadership excellence

(Source: *Good to Great*, 2001)

Humility

Will

Two Leadership Principles in Theory U: Leading with Attention and Intention

Theory U, a recent learning theory of leadership proposed by Otto Scharmer of MIT introduces the simultaneously active and receptive concept of *presencing,* a representation of leadership as a dynamic integrative process and, in this case, integrating both *attention* and *intention* at the intrapersonal and collective levels. Again, two complementary principles.

Scharmer (2009) writes:

> Successful leadership depends on the quality of *attention and intention* that the leader brings to any situation. Two leaders in the same circumstances doing the same thing can bring about completely different outcomes, depending on the inner place from which each operates.

In continuity with systems researchers, Senge, Scharmer, Jaworski and Flowers proposed the concept of 'presencing', which they define "as the capacity to act in a way that actions are born out of the future as it emerges."

Presencing involves enacting what they term three processes of introspective conversions:

1. Shifting from an attitude of judgment to an attitude of exploration.

2. Shifting from avoiding emotions to appreciation, "to see with the heart."

3. Moving from a rigid will of the ego to a more flexible will that is more receptive to the future.

Scharmer and his colleagues propose that leadership can be developed by going through a U-process from observing and receiving information mindfully without judgment, and from that generative listening make meaning and define new possibilities and actions. This U-process is proposed as a generative attentive process that individuals and groups can learn to experience so they can lead change more consciously and creatively, in *dialogue with the universe.*

Table 4, below, highlights the recurring and complementary factors found in leadership theories discussed so far. The following sections of psychology, and ancient philosophies will also highlight similar bidimensional factors, as well as their integrative complementarity, which the latest learning leadership theories also demonstrated.

For a more detailed thematic analysis of 300 leadership characteristics leading to the proposition of *intentionality* and *appreciation* as the yin and yang factors of this model, please read my Ph.D. dissertation: *A Study of the Yin and Yang Model of Leadership for Individual and Collective Leadership Development.*

Table 4: Recurring and complementary factors in leadership theories

YEAR	THEORY	FACTOR 1	FACTOR 2
1950	Trait theories	Task qualities	Relationship qualities
1957	Ohio State University	Initiating structure	Consideration
1964	University of Texas Leadership Grid (Blake & Mouton)	Concern for production	Concern for people
1966	University of Michigan	Job-centered	Employee-centered
1969	Situational Leadership (Hersey & Blanchard)	Task behavior (Guidance)	Relationship behavior (Supportive behavior)
1971	Path-Goal Theory (House)	Achievement-oriented and directive behavior	Participative and supportive behaviors
1975	Systems Theory (Capra & Flatau)	Design	Emergence
1988	Self-directed learning (Kolb Boyatzis)	Protolearning (Intentions that anticipate the future)	Retrolearning (Re-examination and debriefing of past experiences)
2001	Good to great (Collins)	Intense professional will	Deep personal humility
2008	Trait Theory Groupings (Bass & Bass)	Task competence	Interpersonal leadership
2009	Theory U - Presencing (Scharmer, Senge)	Intention	Attention

Bidimensional and integrative representations of leadership in psychology

Two Factors of Leading Self in Psychology

Three perspectives from psychology are also included in this literature review because of their similar bidimensional and integrative definition of leadership at an existential level (i.e. 'How do I lead my existence'), which is also commonly termed as 'Self-leadership'. These are:

1. Carl G. Jung's individuation process with the *masculine* and *feminine* archetypes (1923).

2. Rollo May's existential reflection on *Love and Will* (1969).

3. More recent third-wave cognitive behavioral therapies with the dialectic approach between *non-judgmental acceptance* and *committed action* (Hayes, 2010).

Carl G. Jung and Leading Self with Care and Affirmation

According to psychoanalyst Carl G. Jung, the human quest for human development is not one of achieving perfection but rather one of achieving integration, or wholeness. Jung called the *individuation process* one's unique journey of integrating opposite and complementary principles within oneself.

In his theory of self-leadership, he identifies two key archetypes to integrate:

1) the *Masculine Archetype* (which he refers to as the affirmative principle)

2) the *Feminine Archetype* (which he refers to as the caring principle).

The psychiatrist and Jungian psychoanalyst Anthony Stevens explains:

> The masculine and feminine archetypes are thus psychic structures in all of us. The masculine Yang speaks of an affirmative and active principle, while the feminine archetype Yin notion, speaks of a caring and conciliatory principle.

While earlier behavioral theorists Blake and Mouton (1964) defined good leadership as the ability to be both highly focused on *production* and highly focused on *people*, Jung defines effective self-leading as the ability to integrate both propensities to *affirm* and to *care*. The implications of this psychological perspective for leadership development implies a necessary self-integrating of these two archetypes in oneself in order to lead as an individual. How am I affirming myself in my relationships? And how do I care for others?

Table 5 displays some characteristics which psychiatrist and psychoanalyst Anthony Stevens associates with both the masculine and feminine archetypes.

Table 5: Masculine and feminine
archetype characteristics

MASCULINE	FEMININE
TAKE AND MANAGE POWER	PROTECTIVE
MAINTAIN RULES	EMPATHY
EXPRESS AGGRESSIVITY	NURTURING
EXPERIENCE EMOTIONAL CLOSENESS SIDE-BY-SIDE MORE THAN FACE-TO-FACE	SENSITIVITY TO PERSONAL RELATIONSHIPS
AFFIRMATION	ABILITY TO TALK ABOUT ONE'S FEELINGS FACE-TO-FACE
ACTION- AND FUTURE-ORIENTED	CONCILIATION

Rollo May and Leading one's existence with Care and Will

Building on American pioneer psychologist William James' reflections on the human will, existential psychologist Rollo May (1969) distinguished the 'healthy will' from the Victorian duty-abiding and rationalistic 'will power' or 'willfulness' as well as from the pleasure-seeking 'wishing' or 'craving' characteristic of modern consumer society's perpetual creation of 'wants'.

May presents *intentionality* as an epistemology, a way of knowing, and "structure which gives meaning to experience" (p. 222). By defining what I want to do, I infuse meaning in my action. May echoes psychoanalyst Viktor Frankl's (1955) earlier notion of *proactiveness*, and the importance of intentionality:

> I say that if man is not engaged in making his meaning, he will never know reality... I have emphasized that intentionality contains both our knowing and our forming of reality, and that these are inseparable from each other.

In addition to presenting *will* as an anticipatory, influencing and shaping attitude, May also presents *care* as the complementary principle of *will* and as its actual source. In his words:

> Will is the full-blown, matured form of wish, and is rooted with ontological necessity in care. In an individual's conscious act, will and care go together, are in that sense identical.

Like German philosopher Heidegger's proposition that "willing is caring made free," May suggests that *care* (i.e., attention or appreciation) consequentially elevates human *wishing* to human willing *and* making it an integrative and creative act:

> Hence, I speak of the relating of love and will not as a state given us automatically, but as a task; and to the extent it is gained, it is an achievement. It points toward maturity, integration, wholeness. None of these is ever achieved without relation to its opposite; human progress is never one dimensional. But they become touchstones and criteria of our response to life's possibilities.

According to May, modern man's loss of direction and lack of authentic living is most of all a symptom of his numbness and lack of authentic feeling. It was thus by regaining authentic feeling that modern man could reclaim his own consciousness, authentic meaning and direction. He writes:

> I have long believed that love and will are interdependent and belong together. Both are conjunctive processes of being – a reaching out to influence others, molding, forming, creating the consciousness of the other. But this is only possible, in an inner sense, if one opens oneself at the same time to the influence of the other. And will without love becomes manipulation- of which the age just preceding the First World is replete with examples. Love without will in our day becomes sentimental and experimental.
>
> -Rollo May, *Love and Will*, 1969

Third-Wave Cognitive Behavioral Therapies and Leading One's Life with Acceptance and Commitment

Recent development of third-wave cognitive behavioral therapies such as *Acceptance and Commitment* Therapy (ACT), dialectical behavior therapy, functional analytic psychotherapy, mindfulness-based cognitive therapy and other acceptance and mindfulness-based approaches, have changed the normative cognitive psychotherapeutic approach from eliminating or modifying 'disruptive thought patterns' to welcoming and accepting them, being informed by them, and then leading to more effective change strategies, psychological flexibility and adaptability.

The core therapeutic conception of ACT is that psychological suffering is usually caused by experiential avoidance, cognitive entanglement, and resulting psychological rigidity that leads to a failure to take needed behavioral steps in accord with core values. ACT is proposed as a six-step process that can be summarized by these three points:

1. Accept your reactions and be present

2. Choose a valued direction

3. Take action

ACT has also been adapted to non-therapy training, oriented towards the development of mindfulness, acceptance, and values skills in nonclinical settings such as businesses and schools. This last dialectical approach is another example of a self-integrative perspective proposed for self-leadership.

Table 6 shows the consistent bidimensional and integrative representation of self-leadership in all three schools of psychology in the last century and follows with a section which highlights similar bidimensional and integrative representations of leadership in ancient philosophies.

Table 6: The two leadership factors in psychology

YEAR	THEORY	FACTOR 1	FACTOR 2
1923	Individuation process (Carl Jung)	Masculine archetype (Affirmative)	Feminine archetype (Caring)
1969	Existential psychology (Rollo May)	Will	Care
2014	Third-wave cognitive therapy	Commitment	Acceptance (mindfulness)

Bidimensional and integrative representations of leadership in ancient philosophies

Taoist Philosophy and Leading Change with Yin and Yang

For more than 3,500 years, the Chinese have defined the Taoist notions of yin and yang as two inherent principles that embody the ever-changing flow of life. These notions have been studied and applied to such varied fields as medicine, military strategy, social organization, the arts, and spirituality.

Chinese philosophers consider that leading one's life or any project involves a dynamic managing of these two principles: one of **assertiveness (yang)** and one of **receptivity (yin)**. Limiting oneself to either one of the two principles would be cutting oneself from the dynamic flow of life.

The Confucian understanding of *yi* (intention) is different from its understanding in Western philosophy, according to Ogilvy (2010), as intentionality is not merely projection, but also reflection without the 'aboutness' of intentionality, as suggested by thinkers like Husserl and Brentano.

Confucian intentionality is more closely related with reflexivity. In Confucian cultural psychology, the mind is not merely a passive observer of a situation, nor does it totally invent what it perceives. The Confucian idea of intentionality is a kind of reflective engagement, where people act in and on the world, shaping their experiences according to their own intentions.

The Taoist yin and yang notions exemplify particularly well the integrative perspective of leadership found in many leadership theories in three ways:

1. By highlighting, respectively, the attitudes of assertiveness and receptivity consistently found in leadership theory

2. By showing how these two principles can be dynamically interdependent and mutually related to each other.

3. By revealing how the transformational quality of leadership rests in the dynamic integrative process, in the unifying effect of integrating the two factors.

Figure 3: Two dimensions of leading change in Taoist philosophy

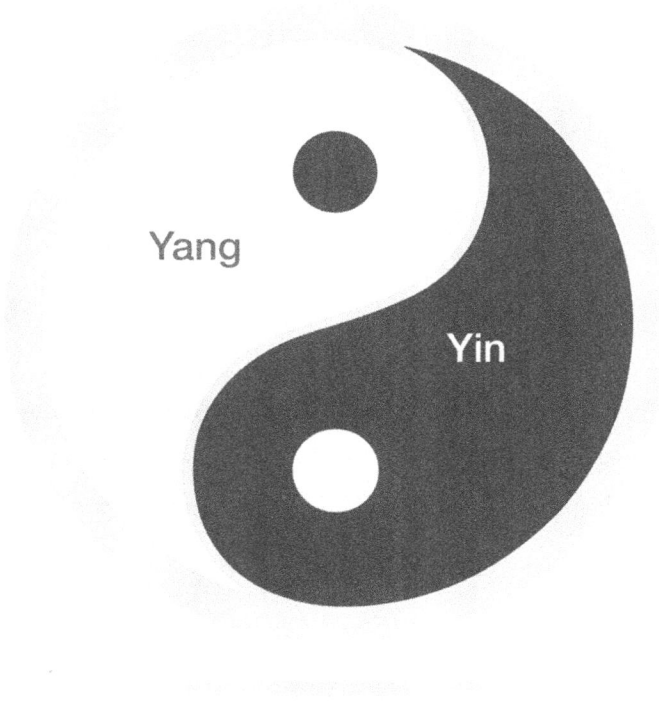

Yogic Philosophy and Leading with
Receptive Listening and Focused Resolve

> Then, one is no longer disturbed by
> the play of opposites.
>
> – *Yoga Sutra* #48

Another nondual eastern tradition worth noting which also presents self-leadership in a bidimensional and integrative way is the yogic tradition, with its notion of leading Self as an integrative process. Yoga is one of the six fundamental systems of Indian thought collectively known as *darsana*, which translates as "a certain way of seeing." Yoga has been systematized as a specific practice by the great Indian sage Patanjali in the *Yoga Sutra,* which is believed to date back to 400 C.E.

Many interpretations of yoga have existed over the centuries, yet one constant interpretation has been the idea of unifying the whole person's mind on one's *sankalpa*, or intention.

The Sanskrit word *sankalpa* has been translated as:

> the idea or notion formed in the
> heart or mind, a solemn vow or
> determination to perform, desire, a
> definite intention, volition or will, a
> determined focus on one's dharma,
> one's deepest intentions, and one's
> qualities of the Divine within.

A *sankalpa* can speak to the existential aspect of our lives: our *dharma*, our overriding purpose for being here, and at a more functional level, it can speak of having *resolve* or a determined intention to accomplish a particular task or objective in one's life. Table 7 presents these two levels of resolve for individuals.

Table 7: Two levels of resolve: existential and functional

TWO LEVELS OF SANKALPA

RESOLVE	INDIVIDUAL
Functional leadership	An individual willing to achieve a personal objective / purpose
. . . . .	. . . . .
Existential leadership	An individual living one's life with a sense of purpose and identity

*Model adapted from the Hindu notion of *sankalpa,* the one-pointed resolve to do or achieve presented with two levels of resolve (originating from the *Rig Veda*).

According to Richard Miller, clinical psychologist and yogic scholar, a *sankalpa* arrives with everything needed to fully realize it. This includes *iccha* (tremendous will and energy), *kriya* (action), and *jnana* (the wisdom of how to deliver that action). Miller writes:

> You don't have to ask where you'll find the will to do it. The energy and will is already there. The *sankalpa* informs us of the action we're willing to take into the world.

Discovering one's Sankalpa with good listening

According to yogic philosophy, the way to discover one's *sankalpa*, or inner will, is through careful listening and creating a calm and still mind in order to hear the divine will within. Miller suggests:

> Your heartfelt desire is already present, waiting to be seen, heard, and felt. It's not something you need to make up, and the mind doesn't have to go wildly searching for it.

Miller describes a three-step process of yogic listening which is again very similar in states and processes to the three levels of appreciative knowing elaborated by Srivastva, Fry, and

Cooperider (1989), as well as Marshall Rosenberg's (1999) three stages of empathic listening.

The three states of yogic listening:

1. *Sravana*: The first state of listening in yogic philosophy, *sravana*, is "the willingness to hear the message of the heartfelt desire."

2. *Manana*: The second state of yogic listening, *manana*, "is the act of turning to and welcoming the messenger in. When you hear the call, you must be willing to sit with it, feel it, and deeply reflect on it."

3. *Nididhyasana*: The final stage, *nididhyasana*, "is the willingness to do what the heartfelt desire requires of you. It will call you into action, into the world," says Miller (p. 26). "You must be willing to respond."

Like Heidegger's notion of 'care' generating conscious willing, yogic listening also leads to intentional action—as if good appreciating leads to good willing.

Management Pioneer
Mary Parker Follett:
Leading as a Process of Integrating

> The power of leadership is the power
> of integrating.
>
> – Mary Parker Follett

All of the approaches mentioned so far, from the first trait and behavioral studies up to the most recent learning theories of leadership, third-wave cognitive psychology, and eastern philosophies, all lead us to a similar understanding of leadership as an integrative process at the individual and collective levels.

Remarkably, this vision was proposed as early as the beginning of the 20th century by Mary Parker Follett (1868-1933), an American woman whose ideas have been considered far ahead of her time. The late management scholar Peter Drucker called Mary Parker Follett "the prophet of management." Leadership scholar Warren Bennis also wrote, "just about everything written today about leadership and organizations comes from Mary Parker Follett's writings and lectures."

Follett viewed leadership as an integrative process. She wrote:

> Business unifying must be understood
> as a process, not a product. We have
> to become process conscious.

Follett proposed a management model she called *power-with* management in opposition to the pervading management model of *power-over*. A leader, according to Follett, didn't impose his or her will, as one would customarily say; leaders, according to Follett, were the ones able to evoke and integrate all the possible influences and powers within themselves and with others in order to cocreate ever greater unified power.

Mary Parker Follett writes:

> Again, our idea of power is changing.
> Men have long worshipped power; the
> power of arms, the power of divine
> right-of kings and priests – and then
> in the nineteenth century the power of
> majorities. Our conception of
> democracy is only to-day beginning to
> free itself from that taint. And the
> reason that it is freeing itself is that
> our idea of power is changing. Power
> is now beginning to be taught of by

some as the combined capacities of a group. We get power through effective relations. This means that some people are beginning to conceive of the leader, not as the man in the group who is able to assert his individual will and get others to follow him, but as the one who knows how to relate these different wills so that they will have a driving Principle. He must know how to create a group power rather than to express a personal power. He must make the team.

– Mary Parker Follett

Follett's notion of power-with was proposed as the German philosopher Martin Buber was writing *I and Thou* in 1923, and distinguishing two modes of existences: *I-IT*, a utilitarian relating with a separate other as an object and *I-Thou*, a mutually influencing relationship with another as a subject. Follett's power-with here also preceded Karl Weick's 1979 notion of *double interacts* (i.e. back-and-forth relationship) as the basic unit of social interaction and key characteristic of leadership as an exercise in power-with and not power-over.

As Weick writes,

> When there is no double interact
> possible (and thus only an interact),
> as in the situation of authoritative
> power or bureaucratic activity, there
> is no open responsiveness and no
> redefinition possible, and the social
> process becomes reified: organizing
> becomes organization.

For Follett, social control and coordination was the fruit of this dynamic integrative process; and group life was the experimental environment for this to take place:

> What then is the essence of the group
> process by which are evolved the
> collective thought and the collective
> wills? It is an acting and reacting, a
> single and identical process which
> brings out differences and integrates
> them into unity. The complex
> reciprocal action, the intricate
> interweavings of the members of the
> group, is the social process.

If servant leadership theory as proposed by Greenleaf (2002) speaks of the leader as being invested of a moral mission to serve others and thus exemplify a particularly people/relationship orientation of leadership, Mary Parker Follett speaks of the leader's moral imperative to serve the integrative process within oneself and with others. As Follett wrote, "It is the very Process itself to which I give my loyalty and every activity of my life." And this process she refers to is the ever-present process of integrating at the basis of leading.

Table 8 below presents an overall chronological listing of bidimensional and integrative representations of leadership which sets the ground for the new yin and yang model and appreciation and intentionality as its two complementary factors.

Table 8: Overall table of bidimensional representations of leadership
in chronological order

1500 B.C	BC Chinese philosophy Taoism	Yang (Initiate)	Yin (Conciliate)
400 CE	Patanjali's Yoga Sutra	Sankalpa (Resolve)	Compassionate Listening
1918	Mary Parker Follett Integrative management	Power	With
1923	Carl G. Jung Self-development and Integration	Masculine Affirmation	Feminine Care
1950	Leadership Trait Theories	Task qualities	Relationship qualities
1957	Ohio State University Behavioral factors	Initiating structure	Consideration
1964	University of Texas Blake and Mouton Leadership Grid	Concern for production	Concern for people
1966	University of Michigan Behavioral factors	Job-centered	Employee-centered
1969	Hersey & Blanchard Situational Leadership	Task Behavior (Guidance)	Relationship Behavior (Supportive Behavior)
1969	Rollo May Existential psychology	Will	Care

1971	Path-Goal theory	Achievement-oriented and Directive behaviors	Participative and Supportive behaviors
1975	Systems theory (Flatau & Capra)	Design	Emergence
1988	Kolb Experiential Learning Theory, Kolb & Boyatzis Self-directed learning	Protolearning the formulation of scenarios, hypotheses, beliefs, and intentions, which anticipates the future.	Retrolearning the re-examination and debriefing of past experiences, establishing general operating principles, adding cumulative quality to organizational efforts and a sense of historical continuity
2001	Good to Great, Level 5 Leadership, Collins	Fierce Professional Will	Deep Personal Humility
2008	Trait theory groupings Bass & Bass	Task competence	Interpersonal leadership
2008	O. Scharmer, O, P. Senge, *et al.* Presencing, Theory U	Intention	Attention
2014	Acceptance and commitment therapy Third-wave cognitive therapies	Commitment	Acceptance (Mindfulness)

Choosing Two Leading Attitudes:
The Yin and Yang Model
of Leadership

Based on this longstanding consistency of bidimensional representations of leadership (read more in Part I), I developed the multi-level **Yin and Yang Model of Leadership** as an integrative model for individuals and collectives and with intentionality (yang) and appreciation (yin) as its two transformational and complementary leadership attributes. Not only do both factors of intentionality and appreciation summarize well the longstanding consistencies of bidimensional factors found in leadership theories and models, but both intentionality and appreciation complement each other in an integrative way.

The Yin factor of Leadership:
From Consideration to Appreciation

The first people to write about the concept of *appreciation* with leadership were David Cooperrider, Suresh Srivastva, and Ron Fry from Case Western Reserve University in the early 1990s. These organization development scholars and pioneers highlighted the generative quality of appreciation as a leadership attitude and particularly its three main effects, which they highlight in their introduction to *The Call for Executive Appreciation (1989):*

> Appreciative knowing is a distinctive experience and cognitive process that simultaneously 1) appreciates, 2) values, and 3) constructs that which has fundamental meaning.

(numerical emphasis added)

Going beyond the reductive 'people factor' label of 'consideration' and highlighting instead the generative and directional effect of appreciative knowing, the model was based on the transforming levels of appreciation, seen here in the context of leading, for individuals and groups: (1) awareness and mindfulness by appraising, (2) positive energy and intimacy/unity by valuing, and (3) purpose and direction by meaning making. (See the three levels of appreciative leading in Table 9, below).

Table 9: Three levels of appreciative knowing

THREE LEVELS OF APPRECIATIVE LEADERSHIP	APPRECIATIVE LEADERSHIP
Appraising (What is it?)	Listening, observing, acknowledging, accepting, without judgment, being open to connect with a situation and people as they are. Being mindful.
Valuing (How is it good?)	Appreciating, valuing and caring for a situation and people as they are. Appreciating as defining what is most important (values). Being grateful. Celebrating. And generating positive energy.
Meaning-Making (How does it inform me/us on what I/we want?)	Finding meaning, appreciating the symbolism, recognizing a sense of direction, opportunity, possibility in relationship to one's intentions.

While the 'consideration' or 'appreciative' factor has often been considered secondary to the 'task/result' factor in leadership culture (Simonton, 2009), it's impressive to discover how generative appreciating can be in terms of leadership. Greater awareness, positive energy, emotional intelligence, meaning, purpose, and direction: appreciation actually sets the footing for effective leading, as you'll see in Parts II and III.

Postmodern leadership, as Boje, Gephart, and Thatchenkery (1995) foretold in *Postmodern Management and Organization Theory*, integrates previously dichotomized or undervalued aspects of leadership, such as appreciation or heart-centered consciousness for example. They write:

> Rationality is pluralized in postmodernism, but it is not extinct. Rather, rationality must take its role alongside other human capabilities, such as love, fear, pain, and hope.

The Yang Factor of Leadership:
From Initiating Structure to Initiating Intention

The proactive notion of *intentionality*, of defining what one wills, or what a collective wills together, has also been highlighted consistently in leadership theories as a directional precursor to action.

Intentionality, akin to appreciation, with its reflective and generative properties, involves choice and consciousness, and has the advantage of applying naturally to both individuals and collectives (i.e. what I will, what we will).

Rollo May highlights in his classic book *Love and Will* (1969), that appreciating, as we saw just earlier, generates meaning, and thus elevates *wishing* to free and conscious *willing*; willfulness or willpower remain more self-imposed as obligations.

Table 10 presents May's distinction of three forms of wanting.

Table 10: Three forms of wanting

THREE FORMS OF WANTING

VICTORIAN WILLPOWER	The capacity to force our bodies against their desire. Rationalization, moralism.
WISHING	The imaginative playing with the possibility of some act or state occurring.
WILLING	The capacity to organize one's self so that movement in a certain direction or towards a certain goal may take place.

From Rollo May's Love and Will, p. 218

As May also writes, wish and will actually act as polarities to be integrated. He writes: "If you have only 'will' and no wish", you have the dried-up, Victorian, neopuritan man. If you have only 'wish' and no 'will', you have the driven, unfree, infantile person who, as an adult-remaining child, may become the robot man."

Wishing and willing concepts are highlighted as complementary by Rollo May and presented side-by-side in Table 11, below.

Table 11: Wishing and willing as polarities to integrate

WISHING	WILLING
Gives the warmth, the content, the imagination, the child's play, the freshness, and the richness to "will".	Gives the self-direction, the maturity, to "wish".
Wishing brings the life-blood, vitality, and continuity to willing.	Willing protects wishing, permits it to continue without running risks which are too great.

In the context of this book, the expressions 'I want' and 'We want' imply the integration of 'wishing' into 'willing.'

Two levels of Intentional Leadership

The intentional notion of this model inspires itself also from the Hindu notion of *sankalpa* or 'resolve' in the sacred Hindu text the *Rig Veda*. As presented in Table 12, intentions can be defined as 'functional,' that is, the intention to achieve a particular task or action. (e.g. I want to achieve this task) and 'existential,' that is, the intention to achieve a particular sense of purpose (e.g. I want to achieve in my life).

Table 12: Two levels of intentional leadership for individuals and groups

TWO LEVELS OF INTENTIONAL LEADERSHIP	INDIVIDUAL INTENTIONAL LEADERSHIP	GROUP INTENTIONAL LEADERSHIP
FUNCTIONAL LEADERSHIP	Willing to achieve a personal objective / purpose.	Willing to achieve as a group the same objective/purpose.
EXISTENTIAL LEADERSHIP	Willing to achieve one's life with a sense of purpose or willful sense of direction.	Willing as a group to achieve one's mission with a sense of purpose and willful sense of direction.

*Model based on the Hindu notion of *sankalpa*, the one-pointed resolve to do or achieve presented with two levels of resolve (originating from sacred Hindu text, the *Rig Veda*).

The Yin and Yang Model:
A Leadership Model Accessible to Every Person, Pair, and Group

The need for individual and collective leadership is becoming more and more vital for contemporary societies. This book offers an integrative leadership model with proven success with thousands of leaders from around the world, that's also accessible to every individual and collective wanting to learn and develop leadership.

Just as modern management pioneers Douglas McGregor and Mary Parker Follett envisioned human organizations as environments where individual and collective purposes could be creatively integrated, this book offers a theoretical and practical guide to better understand and apply leadership at the intrapersonal, interpersonal, and group levels.

Part II: Experiencing the Yin and Yang of Leading as Individuals, following, explores how every person can lead by developing their own intentional and appreciative leadership and that of others. And *Part III: Experiencing the Yin and Yang of Leading as Collectives* explores the same questions for pairs and groups of all sizes.

Figure 4: The Yin and Yang Model of Leadership

as Individuals and Collectives

Intentional
leadership

What I will
What we will together

What I appreciate
What we appreciate
together

Appreciative
leadership

PART II

EXPERIENCING THE YIN AND YANG OF LEADING AS AN INDIVIDUAL

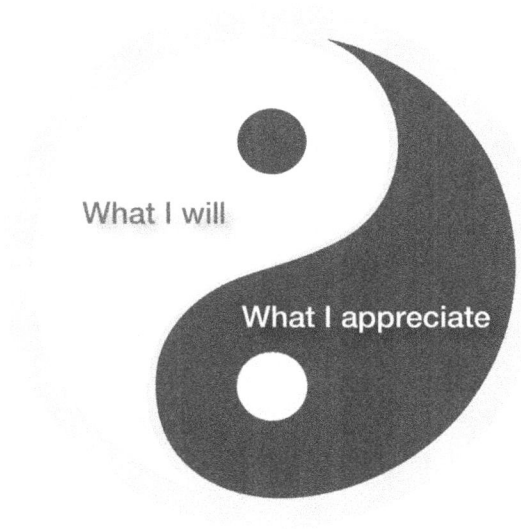

In these two chapters, discover how to experience your own intentional and appreciative leadership as an individual and how to develop it in others.

Love and do what you will.

— Augustine of Hippo

Leading Intentionally as an Individual:
From Initiating Structure
to Initiating Intention

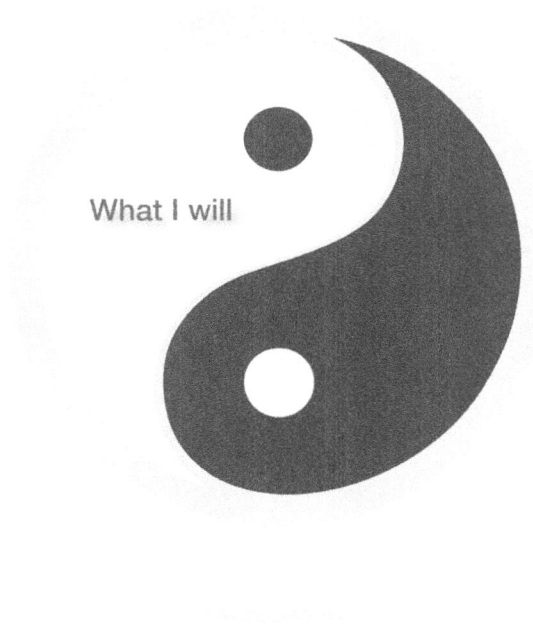

What I will

This chapter explores those moments when leaders initiate,
envision, act, with a unique and unwavering focus on an
objective, a task, a vision, a dream.

The infinite activity of the Power itself is not for its own sake, and as an ultimate end; but it is only for the sake of evidencing, in Intuition, the Being of the Will.

– Johann Gottlieb Fichte

Intentional Leadership and Original Intent

Leadership starts with an intention, and this chapter addresses how leaders lead with original intent, and how unique passions, talents, and aspirations are pathways to intentional leadership.

From the earliest behavioral studies at Ohio State in 1957 to the most recent leadership research today, individual leaders share a sense of *purpose* and *direction*, and act with that in mind. Ohio State university researchers first termed this intentional leadership factor as *initiating structure*, or "the extent to which a leader is task oriented and directs subordinates' work activities toward goal achievement." The leader sets rules and conditions to attain the objective, or the intention.

Today, cognitive versions of the intentional factor of *initiating structure* have been proposed by many leadership researchers, theorists, and authors. Peter Senge in the seminal *The Fifth Discipline* proposes in the early 1990s the learning leadership concept of *personal mastery*, which he defines as "the process of guiding one's actions by continuously focusing and refocusing on what we really want."

Written around the same time as Senge's *The Fifth Discipline,* Stephen Covey's 1990s self-help bestseller *The 7 Habits of Effective People* also presents life leadership as "the capacity to be proactive in defining one's choices and personal priorities. And to give these choices a sense of direction and meaning and to act upon this vision or ideal."

Psychoanalyst Carl Jung also spoke of the Self as "essentially purposive and directed."

> The Self is undoubtedly my origin, but it is also the object of my quest... I have to discover it through my actions, where it first appears wearing singular masks.
>
> – Carl G. Jung

The sum of these ideas is that the quality of one's leadership becomes proportional to one's conscious focusing and refocusing on what one really wants, and ensuring that one's actions are congruently aligned. Jim Collin's Hedgehog Concept in *Good to Great (2001)* is a more recent reminder that leaders distinguish themselves by focusing their efforts on three things:

1. What they're deeply passionate about

2. What they do best

3. What drives their economic engine, as Collins proposes

> Leadership is not about being better than someone else. It's about being unique.
>
> – Robert Lepage,
> director, playwright, actor

Leaders are not only characterized by their intentional nature but by an intentionality that is original. I'm 'leading' when I will what I want to want. Not what others want or certainly not what others think I should want. CEOs or leaders in any area are all at risk of losing their own sense of leadership when they lose sight of their own sense of purpose and direction. The cry for courage and integrity in our organizations is also a call for courage and integrity of each leader with him or her Self.

Psychologist and best-selling author Wayne Dyer writes in the *Power of Intention*: "Envy and greed are symptoms of a lack of original intention." What Dyer, like previous authors, proposes is that authentic leadership starts with a sense of original intent rooted in one's unique talents, passions and aspirations. The careerist, in contrast, lacks leadership, because he or she is overly defined by what the outside world demands (for example, regarding expectations from the family, the social environment, the fashion, etc.): What will others say? What impression will my choices make?

By acting with original intent, a leader develops a true sense of authority (the word 'authority' comes from word 'author'). The leader is thus coauthor of his or her own life by living out his or her own intentions.

Intentional leadership, as we see today, initiates more than structures; it initiates intentions, which then structure their existence and their projects.

Table 12 illustrates two levels of intentionality for individuals and groups in conjunction with the yin and yang model of leadership:

1. A functional level of willing

2. An existential level of willing

**Table 12: Two levels of intentional leadership
for individuals and groups**

TWO LEVELS OF INTENTIONAL LEADERSHIP	INDIVIDUAL INTENTIONAL LEADERSHIP	GROUP INTENTIONAL LEADERSHIP
FUNCTIONAL LEADERSHIP	Willing to achieve a personal objective / purpose.	Willing to achieve as a group the same objective/purpose.
EXISTENTIAL LEADERSHIP	Willing to achieve one's life with a sense of purpose or willful sense of direction.	Willing as a group to achieve one's mission with a sense of purpose and willful sense of direction.

*Model based on the Hindu notion of sankalpa, the one-pointed resolve to do or achieve, originating from the sacred Hindu text the Rig Veda).

Leaders are made, not born, and made more by themselves than by any external means... No leader sets out to be a leader per se, but rather to express him/herself freely and fully... becoming a leader is synonymous with becoming yourself. It is precisely that simple, and it's also that difficult... First and foremost, find out what it is you're about, and be that.

– Warren Bennis,
On Becoming a Leader

The starting point in leadership development is the discovery of who the person wants to be.

– Richard Boyatzis

The Hero's Journey: The Universal Calling to Intentional Leadership

Thomas Carlisle, the late 19th-century writer of the Great Man Theory of leadership, wrote of leaders as predestined individuals able to lead the following masses towards progress. Here's how he illustrates this leader-follower perspective in *On Heroes, Hero-worship and the Heroic in History*:

> For, as I take it, Universal History, the history of what man has accomplished in this world, is at bottom the History of the Great Men who have worked here. They were the leaders of men, these great ones; the modellers, patterns, and in a wide sense creators, of whatsoever the general mass of men contrived to do or to attain; all things that we see standing accomplished in the world are properly the outer material result, the practical realization and embodiment, of Thoughts that dwelt in the Great Men sent into the world: the soul of the whole world's history, it may justly be considered, were the history of these. (1840)

Although Carlisle's belief that leadership belongs to a heroic few is still very present today, the democratic shift of the 20th century in management theory meant an official departure from the Great Man Theory of leadership. It also meant a departure from a caste-like vision of the universe where leaders were an exclusive few who could wield power over the following many to a revision of leadership as the birthright of every free man and woman to self-govern their own existence in freedom, equality and justice. Modern leadership in a democratic world, therefore, meant that heroism had become every person's birthright and destiny.

Mary Parker Follett (1918) writes:

> While therefore there are still men who try to surround themselves with docile servants – you all know that type – the ablest men today have a larger aim, they wish to be leaders of leaders. This does not mean that they abandon one iota of power. But the great leader tries also to develop power wherever he can among those who work with him, and then he gathers all this power and uses it as the energising force of a progressing enterprise.

The hero in every individual

American mythologist Joseph Campbell illustrates in his seminal book *Hero with a Thousand Faces* (1949) how the popular hero myth found throughout human history represents the universal human aspiration for self-realization, and a reminder of how every single person shares this inner yearning to be the heroic leader of their own life. This popularized hero myth used throughout literature (e.g. Ulysses in Homer's epic poem, *The Odyssey*), and in more recent Hollywood movies (e.g. the *Star Wars* franchise, *The Lord of the Rings* film trilogy, the *Harry Potter* films) acts as a universal template describing the leadership journey of human courage and authentic self-expression towards wholeness. In that sense, the heroic myth represents also the heroic character of leadership.

Hollywood has understood well how the universal hero speaks to our basic human quest to become. As we line up to see the next *Harry Potter, Star Wars, Lord of the Rings* or the newest Disney adventure, we anticipate 90 minutes of vicarious heroic adventure. And following Campbell's work, Hollywood has actually been using his Hero's Journey as a template in the movie industry.

Campbell identified 12 key steps on the archetypal hero's journey (see Figure 5). I've adapted the 12 steps into 6 steps for a leader's heroic intentional journey we can all call our own (Figure 6).

Figure 5: The 12 Steps of the Hero's Journey in Hollywood

THE HERO'S JOURNEY IN 12 STEPS

Ordinary world · Call to adventure · Refusal · Meeting with the mentor · Crossing the threshold · Tests, allies, enemies · Approach to innermost cave · Ordeal · Reward (seizing the Sword) · The road back · Resurrection · Return with the elixir

Ordinary world	Special world	Ordinary world
ACT I	ACT II	ACT III

THE HERO'S JOURNEY
IN 6 STEPS

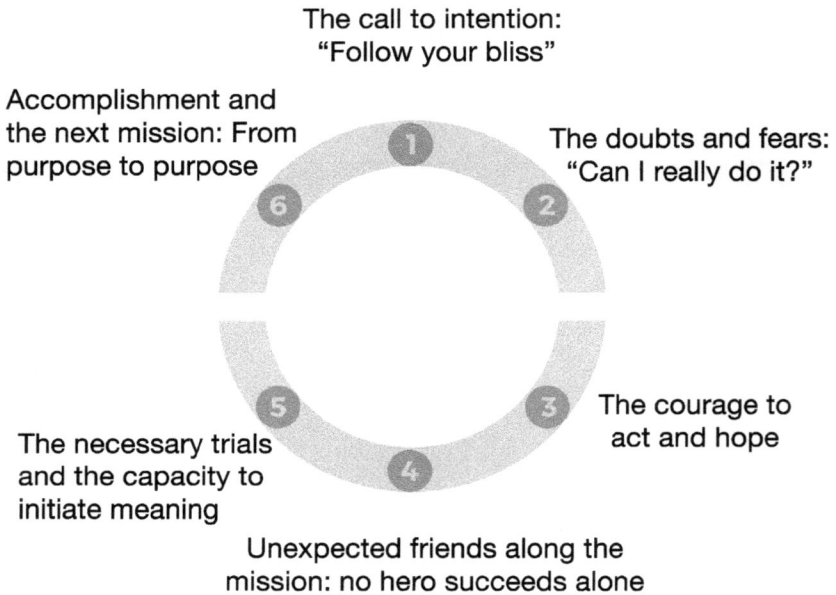

The call to intention:
"Follow your bliss"

Accomplishment and
the next mission: From
purpose to purpose

The doubts and fears:
"Can I really do it?"

The courage to
act and hope

The necessary trials
and the capacity to
initiate meaning

Unexpected friends along the
mission: no hero succeeds alone

Step 1: The Calling of One's Intention: 'Follow Your Bliss'

Every heroic story starts off with an *ordinary* person, in an *ordinary* world, yet called to live an *extraordinary* adventure. A personal calling which Joseph Campbell defined as a calling to follow one's 'bliss.' The hero, like the leader, is driven by a burning passion to produce or to accomplish a task which he or she is most passionate about and that enlivens him or her the most.

Driven by a personal passion, drive, and intention that is truly original and reflective of one's unique Self and sense of identity is often contrary to expected norms. The hero is inevitably called to leave his or her safe and familiar life to embark on an adventure for which there are neither paved roads nor guarantees. The call is not defined by the surrounding society but rather is something deeply individual and linked to one's identity, similar to Jung's 1923 thoughts on the realization of Self: "The Self is undoubtedly my origin, but it is also the object of my quest... I have to discover it through my actions, where it first appears wearing singular masks."

As Senge, Boyatzis, and Covey reminded us earlier, leading one's existence starts by self-appropriating one's identity and sense of individual self. Jung called this the process of individuation—that is, realizing one's full individuality. Living out one's unique passions and talents and finding meaning and fulfillment by making these passions and talents serve with others.

In the search for your own unique vision, you need a different definition of 'genius', one closer to the dictionary definition as 'the unique and identifying spirit of a person or place.' By this definition, your genius consists of those of your talents that you love to develop and use. These are the things that you can now or potentially could do with excellence, which are fulfilling in the doing of them; so fulfilling that if you also get paid to do them, it feels not like compensation, but like a gift.

– Herbert A. Shepard

The drive to excel for a true leader comes from within. The psychologist and humanist Maslow's hierarchy of human needs says the highest level of human motivation is self-actualization that is 'the desire to become more and more what one is, to become everything that one is capable of becoming.'

– Stephen Covey

Don't ask yourself what the world needs; ask yourself what makes you come alive. And then go and do that. Because what the world needs is people who have come alive.

– Kahlil Gibran

Step 2: The Doubts and Fears: 'Can I Really Do It?'

Even though the hero is called to follow his or her bliss, any significant journey has its resistances. Following one's bliss is not easy. Wanting to live one's passion can be exciting… and scary. There is so much unknown. There is the fear of failure, fear of rejection, fear of being different and being alone … Our hero's journey is the road less travelled.

The hero's voluntary answering to the calling is often in of itself a struggle. Although the hero may be eager to accept the quest, at this stage he or she will have fears that need overcoming. The hero may fight thoughts or personal doubts as to whether or not he or she is up to the challenge.

Although doubt can be a sign of significance (i.e., the real journey is scary, and not the easy way), an extreme symptom of resistance to one's own calling will inevitably lead to depression, as it's often the symptom of the depletion of a life's vitality and fire. When you find yourself overly defined by outside norms and expectations or simply disconnected from your own vitality, depressive periods can actually become unexpected opportunities to revisit your life and regain a more complete sense of purpose and self-expression. The energy will follow.

Always in the big woods when you leave familiar ground and step off alone into a new place there will be, along with the feelings of curiosity and excitement, a little nagging of dread. It is the ancient fear of the unknown, and it is your first bond with the wilderness you are going into. What you are doing is exploring. You are undertaking the first experience of our essential loneliness, for nobody can discover the world for anybody else. It is only after we have discovered it for ourselves that it becomes a common ground and a common bond, and we cease to be alone.

– Wendell Berry

Step 3: The Courage to Act and Hope

It's time to speak out, to act, to move forward assertively with determination despite the uncertainty, to step forward, willing this original intention that animates you. The hero and the leader are bearers and stewards of intentions and purposes. They don't let go.

I've always been struck by how leaders work relentlessly and never give up, and I've wondered how they managed to garner such energy. It's not because someone told them to; it's because there was something burning inside of them that they wanted to achieve. No wonder the origin of the word 'courage' comes from the Latin word *'cor'* meaning *heart*.

This sense of perseverance and fierce resolve is characteristic of leadership excellence, according to Jim Collins (2001). But this determination is not an aggressive attitude. It's a confident, determined, and hopeful attitude, in the sense of much more than just wanting something to happen; hope as confidence with a real sense of expectancy, even if something seems impossible to achieve. There are no other alternatives.

What do you have fierce resolve for? What is that dream that you have to protect? And that is calling you? There lies your intentional leadership and the source of your affirmative self-expressive energy.

We need the iron qualities that go with true manhood. We need the positive virtues of resolution, of courage, of indomitable will, of power to do without shrinking the rough work that must always be done.

– Theodore Roosevelt

Happiness is sometimes a blessing but, most of the time, it is a conquest.

– Paolo Coehlo

He who is firm in will molds the world to himself.

- Johann Gottlieb Fichte

Step 4: Unexpected Allies on the Mission: No Hero Succeeds Alone

The more you act on your intention, the more you meet like-minded allies who become partners in the mission. Colleagues, mentors, friends. As much as personal meaning and positive energy is a source of power and vitality, those who share our passions and values are also fundamental to a leader's success. Neither hero nor leader will succeed in isolation or in the company of people who differ in purpose and values.

Leaders are particularly good at appreciating and including the contribution of others, which we'll explore later in the chapter on appreciative leadership.

Step 5: The Necessary Trials and the Capacity to Initiate Meaning

In Tolkien's *The Hobbit*, as in many hero tales, the hero's mission is never easy; and if it is, then it's not the 'real' mission. Whatever the story, the hero's journey is inevitably filled with a multitude of trials and challenges. As fire purifies gold, accomplishing each challenge confirms and reconfirms heroes on their quest.

There are times when the hero must fight for the cause, when it is cold and there is no food, and where neither complaining nor stopping is an option. These necessary challenges pressure the hero to choose and re-choose their mission, reconfirming themselves in the process.

Victor Frankl reminds us in his powerful book and personal concentration camp testimony, *Man's Search for Meaning*, that not only is meaning-making a distinctive human property and basic need but to give meaning to one's situation has dramatic effects on one's reality. It can make the difference between life and death. Man can freely choose his perspective and his attitude towards the inner and outer conditions of his existence. And Frankl believes that one of the main causes of human neurosis in society is man's loss of meaning.

More recently, Thatchenkery and Metzker proposed the notion of Appreciative Intelligence as a capacity to positively reframe situations in ways that helps leaders maintain forward and creative momentum.

Pierre Lavoie, a world-class ironman triathlete champion and household name in Quebec when it comes to public health and exercise, distinguishes Ironman champions from the rest of the pack by their ability to give meaning to the suffering and trials they endure, and to use those situations to motivate themselves even more. Whether it is appreciating the gust of wind as a boost of support to push harder or a head-wind calling him to meet it with any other image that would embolden him, Lavoie argues that it is this capacity to reframe difficult situations into positive perspectives which separates the winners from the rest of the pack. It was this capacity, as it did with Victor Frankl, that enabled him to conquer moments of unbearable suffering during the race and gave him the energy to go beyond his limits in moments of fatigue and discouragement.

What meaning drives you forward in tough times these days?

The probability that we may fail in the struggle ought not to deter us from the support of a cause we believe to be just.

– Abraham Lincoln

Step 6: Accomplishment and the Next Mission: Growing from Purpose to Purpose

The difference between a heroic leader and someone who likes to play celebrity is *service*. Leaders serve a cause beyond themselves. That is the transformational quality highlighted by Bass and Avolio (1997) in their notion of transformational leaders who serve a common vision.

While a narcissistic leader will focus on his or her success and use others as objects for their personal grandeur, a democratic leader, such as one described by Collins' Level 5 Leadership, will serve a shared project and will work to ensure its ongoing success long after their own tenure.

And the story continues from mission to mission: the hero or the leader must also have the courage to continue the journey, to leave the security of the accomplishment and the possible comforts that could numb the will, and undertake the next new adventure towards wholeness. The courage and humility to move on, to leave room for others. The hero's vitality comes from the quest and grows from purpose to purpose. And because purpose is never static as life is never static, the leader re-engages in proactive 'purposing.'

The question now is to redefine it: What do I will today?

True mobility is not about being better than anybody else, it's about being better than the way we were.

– Wayne Dyer

A good hockey player plays where the puck is. A great hockey player plays where the puck is going to be.

– Wayne Gretzky,
National Hockey League legend

Intentional Leadership and Integrity: The Inner Moral Compass

In workshop after workshop, I hear leaders identify their significant leader as someone with a personal ethic, an inner moral compass, a personal discipline, integrity. And in a context where leadership and integrity are perennially questioned with so many of our leaders and institutions, it's good to remind ourselves that leaders truly distinguish themselves by this inner sense of direction and purpose.

According to some scholars, the original root of the word *sin* refers to the idea of missing one's target, like an archer would miss his target. In biblical Hebrew, the generic word for sin is '*het*.' Which means 'to err,' or 'to miss the mark.' And the Greek word *hamartia* (ἁμαρτία) is also usually translated as 'sin' in the New Testament and also means 'to miss the mark' or 'to miss the target.' Based on these definitions, one could say that we actually sin or lack integrity when we lose sight of our target, of our own inner sense of purpose and direction.

In positive psychology, recent focus has been put on distinguishing between the two Greek notions of well-being and happiness: the hedonic quest for happiness through pleasure and the eudemonic quest for happiness through meaning and self-realization. Whereas hedonic happiness is based on experiencing a sense of well-being through good feelings, Eudemonic happiness is based on experiencing a sense of life purpose, challenges and growth. And recent research support the idea that happiness and wellbeing results from the pursuit of pleasure with the development of individual strengths and virtues.

From this perspective, leadership development and integrity imply the capacity for leaders to become truly intentional and self-directed. Whether it's being intentional about how you want to experience your day, how you want to experience your next meeting, or how you want to experience your life. This subservient focus and refocus on one's intentions can be seen as a dynamic pathway to decision-making, integrity, and happiness.

How can I show integrity if I don't know what I will? Or how can we show integrity if we don't know what we will together? To have more integrity, we need more intentionality; and to have more intentionality, we need more leadership.

As long as we keep purpose in both our organizational and private lives, we are able to wander through realms of chaos, make decisions about what actions will be consistent with our purpose, and emerge with a discernible pattern or shape to our lives.

– Margaret J. Wheatley

Each step must be a goal.

- Jacques Chirac

Consulting Anecdote from the field
The Pottery Anecdote

While working on this writing project, I felt the need at some point to take a break from writing and to do something purely physical, with no computer or thinking involved. I registered for a week-long intensive pottery course—yes, a pottery course with clay, a turn-wheel, and a bucket of water, as it's been done for the last 6,000 years of human civilization. While I was supposed to get out of my head and out of 'thinking' mode, this creative experience of pottery surprised me with its first teaching: *"One action, one intention! One action, one intention!"* repeated Catherine, our wonderful pottery teacher. I couldn't believe it. I have to admit I went home that evening and started writing this section which you're now reading.

When you push on clay as it spins on your table, the clay gradually responds. If you don't leave it time to respond, and you follow up with one action after another, hyperactively, then, well, your clay is going to do the hula-hoop and go all over the place with no clear sense of direction. I speak from experience!

Clarity and constancy of intention and attention seem to be as fundamental in pottery as they are to leading.

Two personal exercises from executive leadership workshops to define your own intentional leadership

Exercise #1: Intentionally Leading My Day
My Personal Newscast

I was driving one day to an appointment while listening to the radio newscast. It was an election period and the commentator was describing each candidate's daily schedule of events: "The day of candidate So-And-So will start with a meeting with such-and-such workers ... and then the other candidate Mrs. So-And-So will be visiting this hospital and then this factory..." I stopped for a second, and turned the radio off. And I asked myself the question: What about my newscast? What would be my newscast today? What do I have on *my* agenda? What are my intentions for the day?

Rather than spending these precious minutes listening to what was going to be the official planning of each political candidate, I started to consider my own day. I began to review my schedule. The appointment at 9 am with... the conference call at 11 am with..., and so on. I took the time to visualize each activity by appreciating the stakes involved and clarifying my own intentions and my feelings, as well. It was a time to re-center and re-anticipate what I really wanted from these meetings or these phone calls. A bit like athletes who visualize the course before doing it for real. I discovered that defining my own morning news, my own intentions of the day had surprising effects on the outcome of my day.

What is happening in your day today? And what are you intentional about today? Try it and see!

Exercise #2: The Professional Life-Line Exercise

Leading My Life's Intention

The Professional Life-Line Exercise is an excellent way to find personal meaning through your own life story. Finding out not so much what you want to do in life but what life wants to do inside of you.

1. Draw a horizontal line across a sheet of paper and mark all your work experiences (incl. volunteer work, summer jobs...) from your very first one to the present (like milestones along a road map).

2. Next, identify the experiences you consider to be your most positive ones, those in which you felt the most alive and satisfied with your accomplishments. The highpoints, peak experiences, and memorable moments.

3. Then, identify those experiences you would qualify as least positive or least satisfying.

4. Review your life-line, and ask yourself these questions:

   - What enlivens me most at work (my passions)?

   - What is most easy and fun thing to do (my unique talents)?

- What is most important to me at this time in my life (my values)?

- What are my dreams, goals, or aspirations at this time in my life (my personal vision/direction)?

- Are there any circumstances in my life at this moment that converge with my personal goals and aspirations (e.g. changes in my environment, emerging opportunities)?

- Do I have new insights from this exercise?

Leading Appreciatively
as an Individual:
From Consideration to Appreciation

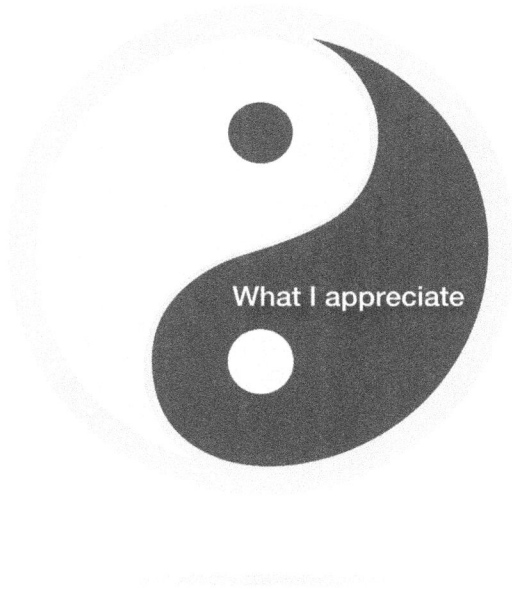

This chapter explores those moments when leaders observe, listen, feel, value, learn, and link it back to meaningful and successful action, and at the same time, help people grow and develop their own leadership.

Much has been said about the need for vision of leaders, but too little has been said about their need to listen, to absorb, to search the environment for trends, and to build the organization's capacity to learn... It seems that the leaders of the future will have to be perceptual learners.

– Edgar H. Schein

While the preceding section on leading intentionally spoke of leadership as the capacity to act with a confident vision and determination, this complementary section on leading appreciatively speaks of a leader's capacity to be open and appreciative of situations and people as they are.

Previously, we looked at the importance of knowing what one wants and making it happen; this chapter looks at the humility of 'not knowing,' of letting things happen, and appreciating the unexpected from people and situations.

The importance today of a leader's humility, attention, mindfulness, emotional intelligence, empathy, listening skills, recognition, presence, awareness, and appreciation of differences are all examples of 'appreciative' leadership qualities. These are probably the most untapped capacities in individual and collective leadership, despite their constant reference since the first behavioral research highlighted *consideration* as one of the two key leader behavioral factors.

This first section addresses the leader's different ways of appreciating *the situation*, and a second section presents different ways of appreciating *people*. And as a reminder, please find the three levels of appreciative leadership presented once again in Table 9.

Table 9: Three Levels of Appreciative Leadership

THREE LEVELS OF APPRECIATIVE LEADERSHIP	APPRECIATIVE LEADERSHIP
Appraising (What is it?)	Listening, observing, acknowledging, accepting, without judgment, being open to connect with a situation and people as they are. Being mindful.
Valuing (How is it good?)	Appreciating, valuing and caring for a situation and people as they are. Appreciating as defining what is most important (values). Being grateful. Celebrating. And generating positive energy.
Meaning-Making (How does it inform me/us on what I/we want?)	Finding meaning, appreciating the symbolism, recognizing a sense of direction, opportunity, possibility in relationship to one's intentions.

Appreciative Leadership as Appraising: Observing and Listening without Judgment

This first level of appreciation can be associated with the idea of appraising or assessing. Paying attention to a situation (or a person) will give you more information than if you were spending the same amount of time judging it and ruminating a perception you already have. Leaders distinguish themselves by their ability to stay open to possibilities where others would not.

Peter Senge (1990) and Otto Scharmer (2009) refer to the capacity to suspend one's judgment and usual critique in order to remain open and allow oneself to be informed by situations. They actually speak of the capacity to be guided by the situation or, as they put it, "to lead as the future emerges;" as if the anticipatory quality of leadership was also an open and receptive attitude. This opening and valuing which can turn the super-natural into The Supernatural.

In the West, you know how to take,
But do not how to receive.

— Indian Teacher

Leading with Ears to the Rail: The Example of Ulysses S. Grant

Although these questions of presence and listening in the act of leading are more contemporary notions of leadership, I was fascinated to discover professor Elizabeth Samet of the US Naval Academy share in *Ears to the Rail: Ulysses S. Grant and the Art of Listening,* how Ulysses S. Grant, the great civil war general and later president of the United States, serves as an illustration of the importance of listening and patient observation in the exercise of leading. Grant was characteristically recognized for his 'Deep Attention,' spending long periods reflecting in silence.

Professor Samet's research on leadership training emphasizes how leadership training activities in the US naval Academy today are meant not so much to train specific areas of competence but instead to build in their officers a personal sense of leadership and capacity to make their own choices in whatever situation.

A leading training officer interviewed by Samet shared:

"I think the most valuable thing I can do is expand an officer's ability to perceive, appreciate, and solve problems. I can't begin to guess what problems they will have to solve. It will be their situation, not mine."

This first level of appreciative listening in leadership is becoming even more important today as we experience a phenomenon French neuroscientist Pierre-Marie Lledo of the Pasteur Institute in Paris calls 'obesity of information, the overabundance of information without the capacity to make meaning out of it. Similarly, Edward M. Hallowell in "Overloaded Circuits: Why Smart People Underperform" (*Harvard Business Review,* 2005), addresses how a new neurological phenomenon called the Attention Deficit Trait (ADT) has now been recognized as the brain's natural response to an overabundance of stimuli and information widely manifest in our hyper-stimulated, modern world.

As much as leadership rests on a dynamic will, philosophers like Aldous Huxley and Rollo May critique modern consumer society with all its noise and distractions, which prevent from silencing the will and truly hearing the purpose calling.

Aldous Huxley and the noisy twentieth century

The twentieth century is, among other things, the Age of Noise. Physical noise, mental noise and noise of desire- we hold history's record for all of them. And no wonder; for all the resources of our almost miraculous technology have been thrown into the current assault against silence. That most popular and influential of all recent inventions, the radio, is nothing but a conduit through which pre-fabricated din can flow into our homes.

And this din goes far deeper, of course, than the ear-drums. It penetrates the mind, filling it with a babel of distractions- news items, mutually irrelevant bits of information, blasts of corybantic or sentimental music, continually repeated doses of drama that bring no catharsis, but merely create a craving for daily or even hourly emotional enemas.

And where, as in most countries, the broadcasting stations support themselves by selling time to advertisers, the noise is carried from the ears, through the realms of phantasy, knowledge and feeling to the ego's central core of wish and desire. Spoken or printed, broadcast over ether or on wood-pulp, all advertising copy has but one purpose-to prevent the will from ever achieving silence. Desirelessness is the condition of deliverance and illumination. The condition of an expanding and technologically progressive system of mass-production is universal craving. Advertising is the organized effort to extend and intensify craving-to extend and intensify, that is to say, the workings of that force, which (as all the saints and teachers of all the higher religions have always taught) is the principal cause of suffering and wrong-doing and the greatest obstacle between the human soul and its divine Ground.

– Aldous Huxley,
Perennial Philosophy, 1946

Appreciative leading is not seeing the glass half-full. It's seeing the glass half-full with water and half-full with air.

Appreciative Leadership Valuing, Caring and Empowering

Valuing, caring, and empowering have been consistently mentioned in leadership theory ever since Ohio State's 'consideration' factor, originally defined as "regarding the comfort, well-being, status, and contributions of followers."

Paying attention makes a big difference in terms of awareness and wellbeing, but paying *positive* attention by appreciating and valuing someone or a situation seems to be even more generative. Appreciation as valuing and offering gratitude generates positive energy and connectedness; it builds trust, cooperative capacity, and innovation. The more we appreciate, the more we develop our capacity to collaborate and our wish to collaborate with each other.

When it comes to associating leadership with appreciation, positive psychology is having a tremendous impact on leadership, as it is in so many other fields such as education, training and coaching today (see more on this topic in the Collective Leadership section with Appreciative Inquiry).

Appreciative Leading and Meaning-Making

The notion of appreciation, like that of consideration, can be interpreted in two ways: first, as *appraising* a person or a situation and, secondly, as *valuing* the same person or situation. I can appreciate how I'm sitting down at my office chair, writing these words on my keyboard, and listening to music in the background, appraising my situation, and become more conscious and connected. I can also appreciate this moment with a deep sense of gratitude of being alive, healthy, and professionally blessed enough to spend time writing this book, which I've dreamt of accomplishing all my life. While the first act I described, appreciating-appraising is more descriptive, the second act of appreciative-valuing brings in an affective dimension.

But appreciation, as a synonym of consideration, also brings a third dimension, which is that of appreciation as *meaning-making*. By appreciating this moment and valuing what it means to me and what it symbolizes, I also generate meaning and direction. Appreciating writing this book also speaks of who I am and what I want to do in life.

As Thatchenkery and Metzker write in *Appreciative Intelligence*, good leaders lead with this capacity to create meaning and positively reframe difficult situations into new opportunities. How can what first appeared to be a problem become a new possibility? Or as my positive psychology friends would remind me, "Say yes to the mess!"

Franco Dragone, a Belgian artistic director who has led projects with Cirque du Soleil and Celine Dion in Las Vegas, offers a creativity lesson on appreciative leadership and appreciating unexpected events. He refers to a personal mantra he uses in times of unexpected changes and frustrations: he puts himself in an inquiring posture and asks himself, "how is this unexpected turn of events a source of new possibility for this project?"

In psychology, we call this cognitive process *reframing*— reevaluating or reperceiving a problem as something that can actually be seen as positive. Instead of perceiving an unexpected change as strictly frustrating (and it can be), Dragone argues that remaining open to work *with* these circumstances often yields much better solutions. Another example of the transformational power of appreciative knowing.

King Solomon and wishing a discerning heart to govern:

At Gibeon the Lord appeared to Solomon during the night in a dream, and God said, 'Ask for whatever you want me to give you.'

'Now, Lord my God, you have made your servant king in place of my father David. But I am only a little child and do not know how to carry out my duties. Your servant is here among the people you have chosen, a great people, too numerous to count or number. So give your servant **a discerning heart to govern** your people and to distinguish between right and wrong. For who is able to govern this great people of yours?'

(cont. on next page)

(cont. from previous page)

The Lord was pleased that Solomon had asked for this. So God said to him, 'Since you have asked for this and not for long life or wealth for yourself, nor have asked for the death of your enemies but for **discernment in administering justice**, I will do what you have asked. I will give you **a wise and discerning heart**, so that there will never have been anyone like you, nor will there ever be.'

– 1 Kings 3:5

Bible New International Version

Consulting Anecdote from the Field

Emotional Intelligence and the Challenge of Naming What We Feel

The starting point of emotional intelligence, and appreciative leadership, is the capacity to perceive and name what we feel. And this starting point of being aware and naming our emotions and those of others is probably the most difficult—but the most crucial—if one is to truly lead with mastery.

What I want to share with you below is a personal coaching anecdote that exemplifies how hard it can be to name an emotion and get a clear sense of what we actually feel in a particular situation. It may take time, different perspectives, and some inner digging and listening to put your finger on it, but naming what we feel is half of the process. Because naming an emotion externalizes it, we can then relate to 'it' and manage 'it' rather than 'it' managing us, as if we have been blindly possessed by some unidentified force.

I'm meeting Steve as part of a series of regular coaching sessions of my leadership program. Steve is an assistant director of field operations at one of Canada's largest airports. His work is to make sure the thousands of kilometers of track and tarmac are always in top quality. The tracks need to be opened and operating 7 days a week whether there's freezing rain or ten inches of snow. Airport personnel from around the world come to learn from Steve's 30-years' experience as a field operations manager and the innovative ways in which the airport has organized track maintenance.

We sit down and I ask Steve, how are you doing? He answers, 'Ok'. Steve is not just an 'ok' kind of person. I notice right away that something's less than normal.

So I ask, are you really ok?

He answers: "I'm tired, irritable. I barked at a few people and I even had to go apologize. I don't know what's happening. I feel like crying. And I don't know why. I don't even know the reason, but I feel this way."

And then he goes on… "I just feel like nothing's moving here. These new kids are in it for a few years, not like what we committed to. They talk about engagement… huh."

I ask Steve what else happened since we last saw each other a few months ago. He adds, "Well, we changed our vice president, which is too bad because I really respected Jim. But he was ready for bigger and better things and I'm happy for him."

Tell me more, I ask. I notice Steve is emotional talking about Jim and I sense this may have to do with his irritability, often a cover-up for sadness. When sadness can't be expressed, it comes out as irritation. Irritability appears as a surface symptom and unconscious self-protection.

As we talk more, I discover that Jim had been Steve's vice-president for the last 20 years. Jim had promoted Steve to manager and had been a mentor and great supporter in the development of first-rate field operations at the airport. Jim had always been attentive to Steve's work and the importance of the quality of the tracks. It was Jim's vice-presidency that invested in building these world-class field operations. He made sure Steve had the best equipment to do the job. And he also knew when it was time to share the praise. This is how Steve, a high school graduate, became recognized around the world as the manager of these reputable field operations. Steve adds, "You know, it's not as if I'd see Jim or talk to him that much, but he was always genuinely interested in doing whatever it took to make the job the best it could be. Once in a while, I'd get a phone call from him somewhere as he was flying back from a business trip. He'd say something like, 'Hey Steve, I'm coming in from Chicago and I hear there's snow, I hope the tracks are good?' We'd chat a bit and you could be sure the tracks were as dry as a baby's bum!" And with that, Steve started to shed a few tears.

Steve had just become conscious of the emotions of grief for the vice president and mentor he cared for, which had been covered up as fatigue and irritability. His sadness was actually grieving the loss of his dear boss and guide, but he just hadn't been able to name the emotion. I say, "It sounds like you're grieving Jim; and grieving takes time." Steve nods affirmatively. Despite the fact that Jim had left two months previously, Steve hadn't known that this was the real reason he was feeling so irritable. But now he knew. He learned that grieving, like any emotion, is unique to each person and takes its own time.

Steve was no longer going to bite anyone, because he was emotionally intelligent now. He perceived and named the real feeling that had been underlying his outward irritability.

The difficulty of appreciating and naming emotions and being emotionally intelligent shows how important personal rituals are, and how necessary it is to take time to make meaning out of our emotional responses.

Again, it's often simply by appreciating a situation and voicing our thoughts that we can find out our own meaning.

Shifting from Reactivity to Appreciative Leadership and Emotional Intelligence

Appreciative leadership and Emotional intelligence is about being able to name what we and what others feel, so that we can then choose to manage and act upon those situations with integrity.

However, as humans, we're all at risk in situations of perceived fear or insecurity of being hijacked by those fears and insecurities and regress to more primitive cognitive states of survival: fight, flight, or freeze. When we're triggered in those perceived situations of threat and insecurity, which may be quite mundane, emotional intelligence and appreciative leadership come to the rescue to chill us out, choose an inquiring mode rather than a judging one, and spend more time seeking the silver lining than elaborating inner theatricals of our own super-ego story.

The plane is delayed, the check bounced, the contract is cancelled. With any unexpected situation that is different from what we want or expect, our way of appreciating and responding to the situation determines how we lead that situation and influence others in the process.

Table 13 shows how you can choose to move from emotional reactivity (on the left), our typical animal-fear-based way of reacting, to appreciative leadership and emotional intelligence (on the right).

Table 13: Emotional reactivity and appreciative leadership

Emotional reactivity	Emotional intelligence/ Appreciative leadership
React against an unexpected and unwanted change in a situation	Try to appreciate an unexpected and unwanted change in a situation as it is
Judging and critical posture	Appreciative inquiring posture
No way! What the...?!	*What's happening?*
Continue to react with strong negative emotions against the situation	Even though the change may be frustrating, suspend pre-conceptions and judgements to experience a more direct contact with reality
Attribute bad intentions Blaming and victimizing (Who's fault is it?)... Finding the scapegoat to punish	Depersonalize the situation and focus on facts and feelings (my own and that of others). (Stay aware and nonreactive)
Repeat usual patterns of response and judgements about the situation	If I can't change the situation, can I change the way I see the situation? This process of choosing a different perspective that changes our relationship with the situation **"re-framing"** *Can a problem become an opportunity?*

Power-over battle	Power-with management and seeking integration
(Us vs. Them)	(Us with the situation, with Them)
Emotional and functional dead-end	Emotional mastery and psycho-logical flexibility.
	Working 'with' the situation and lead the way towards new alternatives which in the end often produce better results than originally planned.

Try This!

Appreciative Leadership and Time-Outs to Appreciate and Renew One's Intentions

Leaders create their own intentions, and they also create their own reflective times to define those intentions.

Here are some examples of reflective practices from leaders I met through my consulting practice that I hope can inspire you to create your own.

- The CEO of a large bank once shared with me how, when faced with difficult decisions, she likes to call a few trusted advisers to just listen to their perspectives, to see what emerges, and to give herself some time to think.

- The CEO of a global IT company holds his own weekly intention-setting meeting. Every Sunday night, he takes a moment to envision his upcoming week and defines his core intentions and priorities for that week. Every choice of activity is subsequently taken with these intentions in mind. Interestingly, this fundamental practice of his was to keep fine-tuning what he called the 'next-step mentality' of leadership: taking time to appreciate in order to better anticipate.

- A plant manager starts every day with a 45-minute round of greetings around the plant. As he says, 'those 45 minutes of greetings and just listening tell me exactly what the challenges of the day will be.'

- Why not make it simple and review the daily thread of your day and identify the aspects you most appreciated and are most grateful for? Or count your blessings, as Steven Covey noticed highly effective people do. You'll see that identifying those things you most appreciated in your day will generate more awareness, positive energy and direction on how you want to lead tomorrow.

- Distinctive personal passions are sources of personal vitality for everyone. They're also privileged moments for meditative thinking to make our own emotional and rational sense of things. What are your personal times to renew your energy and your own meaning?

He who is not master of himself,
Why should he be of another?
Be first master of yourself,
And do what you need.
Then it will be good that you
command.

>   – Gil Vicente, 1465-1536

What I Appreciate of People

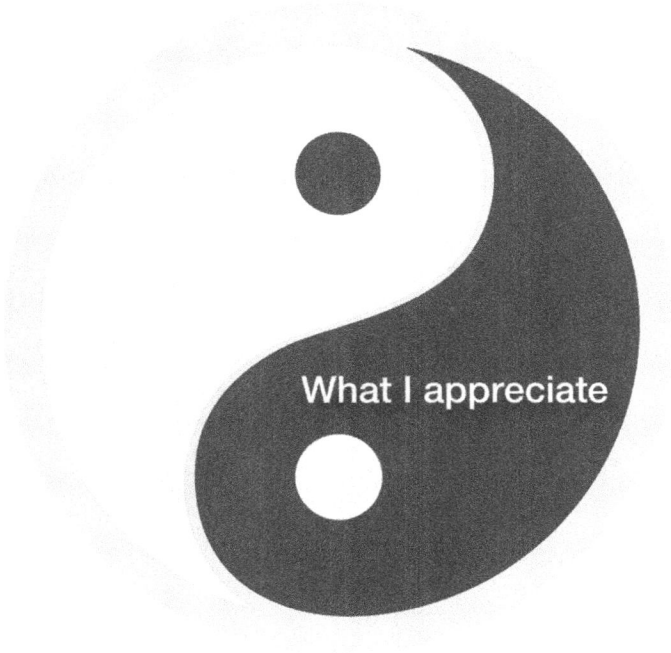

What I appreciate

He is a leader who gives form to the inchoate energy in every man. The person who influences me most is not he who does great deeds but he who makes me feel I can do great deeds.

Many people tell me what I ought to do and just how I ought to do it, but few have made me want something.

Whoever has struck fire out of me, aroused me to action which I should not otherwise have taken, he has been my leader.

– Mary. P. Follett

Leadership and Recognition: The Capacity to Evoke the Best in People

When workshop participants are asked to look back on their own experiences and to identify their most significant leader in the Significant Leader Exercise, these are the things I keep hearing year after year:

- "My best example of leadership was someone who saw and recognized qualities in me that I wasn't even aware of. He made me see them, challenged me to develop them, and helped me believe in my potential. I wouldn't be who I am without this leader, who valued my potential."

Or:

- "This person is my inspiration as a leader because her openness and appreciation allowed me to accomplish things I'd never have been able to achieve otherwise. She valued me for who I was and gave me confidence."

I could go on sharing many other stories like these ones. 'Human' talents are particular, in that the more you see and recognize them, the more they develop.

Recognition and The Hawthorne Effect: "The Mere Fact of Paying Attention"

Harvard psychologist Elton Mayo conducted the now famous Hawthorne Electric Studies in 1956, in which he and his team unexpectedly discovered that "the mere fact of paying attention" to the plant workers under study was a factor in their motivation and increased productivity. While the studies had been designed around the intensity of lighting in the plant, the researchers discovered that the increase in productivity was directly associated with the experimenters' interest in the workers before manipulating the lighting.

Recognition and the Pygmalion Effect

The power of recognition has also been powerfully demonstrated in social studies on the positive Pygmalion dynamic. Originally conducted with rats, and later with humans, these studies led subjects to believe that some of the subjects had exceptionally high potential compared to their siblings (with no other significant difference between them). They studied whether the positive expectancy of the subjects could influence the subjects in their performance. The Pygmalion dynamic experiments showed over time that the correlation between an individual's expectation and the subject's achievement was higher than almost any predictive achievement measure.

The correlations in numerous studies ranged from 0.5 all the way to an almost perfect 0.9. Translated to leadership, these results say that a person's positive expectations of another (i.e., his or her positive perceptions or appreciation of that person's talents) is likely to have a higher correlation with the person's performance than most predictive measures and exercises administered for that candidate's selection.

People who appreciate the qualities we bring to work and believe in our potential act as mirrors—and, even better, as catalysts—for our development. Being recognized makes us aware of our talents, and gives us the confidence and ownership to develop them. Much more than being nice, recognition becomes a developmental act.

Recognition and NBA performance

Credit: Richard Burdett

Steve Nash, NBA two-time MVP and 'master at valuing others,' illustrates a good example of how good leadership is about appreciating those around you.

I once heard Nash in a television interview on PBS where the interviewer, Charlie Rose, asks Nash how he would describe his leadership on the court. And in the most candid and humble manner, Nash starts saying that he tries to build on his teammates' self-esteem. He'd have one of his teammates perform a particular move that was that person's best move. Next, he'd set up another play that would build on another teammate's particular talent. He'd try to build on each one's strengths, and, as he said, everybody then starts to see each other as good and play better.

What strikes me in Steve Nash's story is how one of the greatest NBA players and two-time Champion League Most Valuable Player is the most valuable player at making others feel most valuable.

(See the broadcast: https://charlierose.com/videos/11275, Charlie Rose 08/27/2007)

Recognition Helps Us Make Meaning of Our Own Talents

When others recognize our personal strengths, they're often speaking of our *unique* talents. It can be insightful, when we think about own career orientation, for example, to ask colleagues and close friends what they see as our distinctive qualities and talents. Recognition in these circumstances becomes more than just a sign of kindness; it becomes a door to greater self-knowledge, self-expression, and meaning.

Why not turn your next 'evaluation' meeting into an 'evolution' meeting? Highlight the strongest qualities and achievements of people and see how those particular aspects give meaning and direction to their own leadership. Where do they want to go next?

Leading is putting people in a
position they can grow.

— Workshop participant

William James on Appreciation

Below is a letter from American pioneer psychologist and philosopher William James to his students at Harvard's Radcliffe College, on his discovery of the psychological importance of appreciation.

Cambridge, Apr. 6, 1896

DEAR YOUNG LADIES – I am deeply touched by your remembrance. It is the first time anyone ever treated me so kindly, so you may well believe that the impression on the heart of the lonely sufferer will be even more durable than the impression on your minds of all the teachings of Philosophy 2A. I now perceive one immense omission in my Psychology – the deepest Principle of Human Nature is the craving to be appreciated, and I left it out altogether from the book, because I never had it gratified 'till now. I fear you have let loose a demon in me, and that all my actions will now be for the sake of such rewards. However, I will try to be faithful to this unique and beautiful azalea tree, the pride of my life and delight of my existence. Winter and summer will I tend and water it – even with my tears. Mrs. James shall never go near it or touch it. If it dies, I will die too; and if I die, it shall be planted on my grave.

Don't take all this too jocosely, but believe in the extreme pleasure you have caused me, and in the affectionate feelings with which I am and shall always be faithfully your friend,

Wm. James

Someday, after mastering the winds, the tides and gravity, we shall harness for God the energies of love, and then for a second time in the history of the world, man will have discovered fire.

– Pierre Teilhard de Chardin

Love is what I need to help me know my name.

– Seal, singer/songwriter

I don't like that man.
I must get to know him better.

– Abraham Lincoln

Appreciative Leadership and One-On-One Coaching

Early on in my career as a psychotherapist, I had the chance to be supervised by Jan Bauer, a very talented clinical psychoanalyst, when I decided to get additional clinical training. Jan said something then that has stayed with me to this day.

> She said, "Whatever you do, remember that if you can't love your client, then don't expect them to get better."

The unconditional acceptance, care, and even the love, of the therapist towards the client is a factor of development.

What she meant by 'love' was taking clients seriously in their difficulties, respecting them as individuals, even in their anxieties, and treating them as people who have the right to be understood, not blamed and changed to satisfy other persons. All these are the ingredients of true parental love (*agape*, not *eros*) that we find in the caring of a coaching and a leadership relationship.

The Yin and Yang of Coaching: A Two-Step Process

The appreciative and intentional principles can also be used as a simple and effective coaching framework. A coaching session you can lead on your own by simply structuring your meeting in these two phases:

1. An initial appreciative phase of questioning, inquiring, probing, feeling, exploring, and finding meaning progressively. Listen!

2. A second intentional phase of the coaching based on the meaning generated in the first phase that focuses more on the future: envisioning the ideal solution, next steps and actions to make it happen.

Leadership author Richard Boyatzis proposes two complementary coaching orientations which he calls *coaching with compassion* and *coaching for result;* the appreciative and intentional principles can thus serve as a framework for coaching and leadership development that is both empathic and results-oriented.

The Recognition Letter Exercise

One way of identifying those talents that distinguish us the most is to gather appreciative feedback from people who know us well.

The Recognition Letter exercise consists of inviting people whom you trust, to give you their perception of your personal qualities or particular talents, in the form of an email or a letter.

Send your request in writing to five people you respect and who know you well. These people can be friends, family members, co-workers, classmates; people who have seen you demonstrate your skills over time. It's better to customize each request so that it fits with the specific context of every relationship. It's also important to present a deadline for the response. Use the template on the next page.

Synthesis

Next, identify what emerges in common, the recurring themes between your five letters of recognition. What are the main talents or distinctive qualities that we attribute to you? How does this inform you about your dreams, your intentions?

Adapted from: "Unique Ability: Creating the life you want," Nomura, C & Waller, J., The Strategic Coach (2003), Toronto.

Here's a template you can use:

Hi [Name],

I'm currently doing a professional development exercise that involves asking feedback from people who know me well on what they perceive are my most distinguishing talents.

I'd like you to answer this question:

> *"In light of what you know of me, and thinking back to concrete situations where you saw my contributions make a particular difference, what would you say are the talents or personal qualities that characterize me the most?"*

The exercise guidelines require that your comments refer to concrete situations, supporting your perceptions with examples you remember in order to avoid generalities.

Thank you for your thoughts, I think highly of your opinion.

Could you please return your feedback before [date].

Thanks!

Discussion Part II:
Evolving from the Alpha Boss to the Alpha-Omega Leader:
From Dominating to Integrating

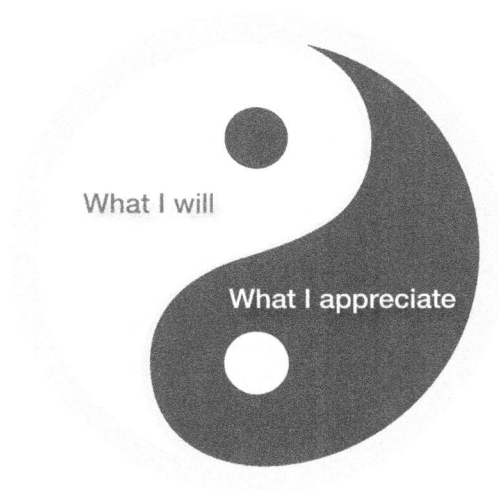

The process of becoming a leader is much the same as becoming an integrated human being.

– Warren Bennis,
Integrative Leadership

Evolving from the Alpha Boss to the Alpha-Omega Leader: From Dominating to Integrating

In this post-modern social and economic world, self-integration, or integrative consciousness, is a critical component of leadership, according to leadership scholar Chleo Akrivou. Because of this, there should be more given to creating leadership development and educational frameworks that make it easier to develop integrative leadership.

Some believe that leadership development efforts should be much less concerned with teaching knowledge and capabilities associated with leadership per se and much more focused on the leader's own process of personal development.

The advantage with the Yin and Yang Model of Leadership is that the conscious development of Self can be developed with both appreciative and intentional leadership principles at the same time. The appreciative and intentional attitudes summarize well the consistent bidimensional factors and at the same time answer the need for a more dynamic and process understanding of leading.

The Yin and Yang Model also frees us from the alpha-male perversion of leading as dominating by proposing an integrative process that every person, man and woman can and should be engaged in to become true leaders of their own lives and projects. A call for integration in each one of us.

A Dynamic Approach to Ethics and Integrity

The Yin and Yang Leadership Model addresses questions of decision-making and integrity for individuals and collectives, and reframes this important question as a process of continuous unifying. Unifying, because pathological living systems, whether they are individual or collective, lack the unifying circulation between polarities and the adaptive flexibility to maintain integrity in changing environments. Many leadership workshop participants have appreciated the Yin and Yang Leadership Model as a 'double-centering' or 'self-tuning' practice, where both appreciative and intentional attitudes act as 'centering' attitudes.

By admiring and following the "strongest person" as leader and choosing these individuals for their singular 'power-over' capacities, we create a false sense of security and dependency for ourselves; And then we're surprised when these power-over champions fall into disgrace after abusing of that same power-over dominance we admired and selected them for.

The Yin and Yang Leadership Model is based on a power-with orientation, which sets a framework for co-creative and interdependent dynamics and thus considers leadership as an integrative function more than a dominating or coercive one. From this perspective, integrity is dialogical and relational. And the model offers a framework to support this dialogical process of integrating to take place individually and collectively.

Power, the desire to achieve one's purpose, and love, the urge to unite with others are actually complementary. As Dr. Martin Luther King Jr. put it, 'Power without love is reckless and abusive, and love without power is sentimental and anemic.'

– Adam Kahane, *Power and Love*

Consulting Anecdote from the Field
Embodying the Yin and Yang of Leadership

If we consider the act of leading one's life or any project as embodying both intentional and appreciative attitudes, I wondered if using somatic exercises could be an effective way to help individuals gain better awareness and self-insight into their own rapport to each of these two leadership postures.

I experimented this on five different occasions with two different yoga instructors, Amélie Bélanger in Montreal and Regina Radisic in Turks and Caicos. Four groups (seven people in each group) were from the general public and one group of 25 were lead oncology nurses. All experimented my corporate leadership workshop based on the Yin and Yang Leadership

Model and each workshop lasted between 90 minutes and three hours in total.

After the usual introductory discussion around the *significant leader exercise˄,* from which we identified the two clusters of yin and yang leadership characteristics, we worked on two sets of exercises, one yin and one yang, followed by personal reflection and a shared discussion.

One set of exercises involved the capacity to envision yourself holding a pose for a long period of time despite the inevitable discomfort and pain. This yang-like exercise called upon the grit to hold the pose, to stick with it, and not let go… The second set of exercises involved relaxing, calming the mind, appreciating, and letting go.

As simple as these exercises and principles were, the somatic insights were powerful for many, myself included. Some of us realized we were quick to let go and wouldn't be forceful enough, whereas others were simply unstoppable and wanted more challenge.

When the participants were asked what they thought of this bidimensional presentation of leadership with the appreciative and intentional principles, here are some examples of what they replied:

- "I found the topic very interesting and useful most of all. It was relevant to me and my husband in terms of putting certain things into action, but also in terms of being able to observe leadership from a more informed perspective."

– Yoga couple

- "I liked the summary table used during the course. I learned theoretical notions about leadership, which I appreciated."

– Member of the general public

- "The two key polarities were clear, and they were presented and explained from many scientific domains."

– Member of the general public

- "The workshop you offered put me in touch with a new dimension of my yin (awareness, recognition) and is certainly what will remain a take-away, a point of profound change, a kind of 'fine tuning', as a gift, a treasure I now take out occasionally since Sunday to watch again and understand better..."

– Yoga teacher

- "I found the workshop very interesting. It highlighted how I've evolved in terms of humility, which I knew was an issue considering my somewhat dominant personality."

– Member of the general public

- "I really became aware of dimensions of my being that still remain to develop, and also my limitations. The explanations were very clear with very respectful feedback."

– Member of the general public

- "The aspects you combined together allowed me to get me out of my head and connect with my body, my heart, my feelings, and my intuition, so my answers were more clear and complete."

– Oncology nurse

- "The somatic exercise dimension allowed me to understand how we embrace our two poles and what importance we give it in our own lives."

– Oncology Nurse

Based on my doctoral research, the 661 participants (i.e. 90 yoga teachers and practitioners, oncology nurses, adults from general public, 90 IT vice presidents, 500 IT managers, and 12 French CEOs) who experienced the Yin and Yang Leadership Model workshops unanimously appreciated the relevance and accessibility of the model as an easy-to-use 'self-assessment' or 'double-centering' model.

(See Appendix A for corporate in-house evaluations that show the relevance and usefulness of the model in different setting).

How are your Systolic and your Diastolic Leadership Pressures Today?

One analogy I like to use to explain the dynamic quality of appreciative and intentional leadership is by comparing them to blood pressure. It's simple to understand and is easy to apply individually and collectively.

There are two measures of blood pressure, the **systolic pressure** (the pushing pressure of the blood flow) and the diastolic pressure (the dilating and relaxing of arteries in order to fill-up with new blood). Both can be used to explain the two complimentary principles of leadership.

1. **Systolic Leadership Pressure**

   The passionate and confident vision, drive, and sustained determination to achieve something you or your collective wants. Without this systolic leadership pressure, without a forceful genuine intent, you are flat or simply going with the current without any self-directed impulse.

2. **Diastolic Leadership Pressure**

   The 'opening' and 'appreciating' to new ideas, new relationships, new feelings, that bring new energy and renewed direction as to what you want now. Without diastolic leadership pressure, we act as a closed-system and are dry of new possibilities.

'Leadership' is consistently presented as integrating two complementary principles, whether we look at it from the point of view of the original Ohio State behavioral studies in 1957 or more recent Theory U in 2009 or Paradoxical Leadership Theory in 2010. The systolic and diastolic analogy is yet another good representation of this consistent leadership pattern, one we experience in our own lives.

When you get up tomorrow morning, why not try this?

Self-assess how are your systolic and diastolic leadership pressures. Jot down your results on the following page. You can make this exercise a regular one throughout the week or month.

Check your systolic leadership pressure:

1. 'Do I know what I want to achieve today?'

2. 'How much systolic push do I have for what I will today?'

Also check your diastolic leadership pressure:

1. 'What am I feeling, thinking, experiencing this morning? Am I connected 'with' the moment and the

experiences of the morning, or am I swimming against the current?'

2. 'Am I feeling grounded and connected with what I want to accomplish today?'

Here is a self-assessment diagram you can use.

SYSTOLIC LEADERSHIP PRESSURE

-1 0   1   2   3   4   5   6   7   8   9   10   11

Deflated   Flat   Intentionally focused   Radically intentional

DIASTOLIC LEADERSHIP PRESSURE

-1 0   1   2   3   4   5   6   7   8   9   10   11

Closed   Open and receptive   Radically appreciative
of the situation and
people as they are

Four Questions To Ask Yourself

1. How radically intentional and radically appreciative am I today?

2. How much am I pushing for what I want to make manifest?

3. How much am I open and appreciating what is?

4. How aware and connected am I to what surrounds me?

Your notes:

PART III

EXPERIENCING THE YIN AND YANG OF LEADERSHIP AS A COLLECTIVE

What we will

What we appreciate

While leadership depends on depth of conviction and the power coming therefrom, there must also be the ability to share that conviction with others, the ability to make purpose articulate. And then that common purpose becomes the leader. And I believe that we are coming more and more to act, whatever our theories, on our faith in the power of this invisible leader. Loyalty to the invisible leader gives us the strongest possible bond of union, establishes a sympathy which is not a sentimental but a dynamic sympathy.

– Mary P. Follett

Leading Appreciatively
as a Collective

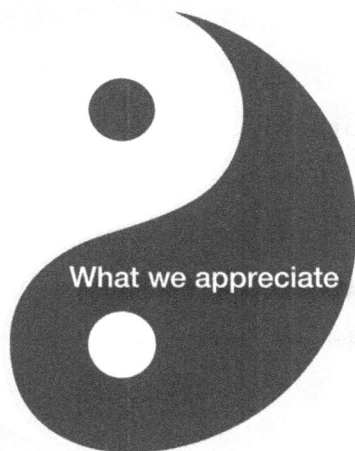

This chapter illustrates the many benefits that appreciative leadership brings to any couple and group, including collective awareness, intelligence, emotional wellbeing, connectedness, ethical behaviors, and the ultimate goal of any collective enterprise: unity of action.

The executive vocation in a post bureaucratic society is to nourish the appreciative soil from which affirmative projections grow, branch off, evolve, and become collective projections. Creating the conditions for organization-wide appreciation is the single most important measure that can be taken to ensure the conscious evolution of a valued and positive future.

– David Cooperrider

As a reminder: Table 9, The three levels of Appreciative Leadership, adapted from Srivastva, Fry and Cooperrider (1989):

THREE LEVELS OF APPRECIATIVE LEADERSHIP	APPRECIATIVE LEADERSHIP
Appraising (What is it?)	Listening, observing, acknowledging, accepting, without judgment, being open to connect with a situation and people as they are. Being mindful.
Valuing (How is it good?)	Appreciating, valuing and caring for a situation and people as they are. Appreciating as defining what is most important (values). Being grateful. Celebrating. And generating positive energy.
Meaning-Making (How does it inform me/us on what I/we want?)	Finding meaning, appreciating the symbolism, recognizing a sense of direction, opportunity, possibility in relationship to one's intentions.

Group Leadership versus Crowd Followership

As we explore collective leadership, it's important to clarify the confusion on the nature of leading with others. In the context of democratic leadership, we have to start by first distinguishing between *crowd collective behavior* and *group collective behavior*.

Groups can either drag us down to animal-like levels of groupism, crowd behavior, governed by conformity, imitation, and suggestion or, groups can make us more creative, adaptable, intelligent, interconnected and alive.

The famous social psychology studies of Asch (1955) on conformity and social pressure, and Milgram (1963) on obedience to authority, have shown all too well how easily humans can be brought to extreme levels of conformity and obedience, even if it means doing harm to a fellow human being that has done us no harm.

Wilfred Bion (2013), British psychoanalyst and world reference on group psychology, also spoke of the risk for task groups of being driven by an unconscious group phenomena he called *basic assumptions*. He defines this as "unconscious group processes which can be seen as a substitute for thinking." Bion's basic assumption 'dependency,' for example, is an unconscious attempt to escape into the safety and subservience to a single leader. We often see this with very assertive leaders who enjoy associating themselves with more dependent individuals, or cultures that favor more authoritarian styles of leading, like a patriarch and his children, for example.

This is where democratic leadership parts from authoritarian leadership, in developing free and creative interdependencies rather than conditioned dependencies. There is nothing wrong in dependency in and of itself, but if there is dependency, a democratic leader will try to make it evolve towards greater interdependency, ownership and leadership—a one-step-at-a-time, continuous and deliberate empowerment of others.

Mary Parker Follett, before her time, also distinguished what democratic leadership could look like, as opposed to conventional power-over authoritarian leadership.

This means that some people are beginning to conceive of the leader, not as the man in the group who is able to assert his individual will and get others to follow him, but as the one who knows how to relate these different wills so that they will have a driving force. He must know how to create a group power rather than to express a personal power. He must make the team. The power of leadership is the power of integrating. This is the power which creates community.

– Mary Parker Follett

For Follett, group psychology—not crowd psychology—was the active pathway towards new democratic living and greater autonomous self-government and human creativity:

> All our ideas of conscious self-determination lead us to a new method: it is not merely that we must be allowed to govern ourselves, we must learn how to govern ourselves; it is not only that we must be given 'free speech', we must learn a speech that is free; we are not given rights, we create rights; it is not only that we must invent machinery to get a social will expressed, we must invent machinery that will get a social will created.
>
> – Mary Parker Follett

Reciprocal Leadership to Be Learned

Late French scientist and humanist Albert Jacquard (2005) calls for a "democracy of ethics" based on our human capacity to define together what is good and desirable. Jacquard states:

> Being superhuman is not about being a single superman, it's about becoming super human when humans come together.

The capacity to lead by creating shared intentions can lead to masterpieces of harmony and beauty.

Orchestra conductor Jean-Marie Zeitouni (2008) chooses to lead differently than in the traditional ways of maestros by favoring a style of leadership he describes as an 'exercise in two movements.' As the conductor, he first defines his own interpretation of the piece. Then, at rehearsal with his colleagues, he remains open to enrich his vision with various ideas and contributions. Step by step, a group alchemy develops, as different changes and adaptations are included. This gradual process progressively builds up to a final interpretation, which has then become a cocreation, a shared accomplishment much richer than the conductor's original vision, and one in which everyone feels part and contributor.

In a more corporate context, a CEO recently confided in me her disappointment about her management team: "They don't say anything; I have to decide everything," she complained. "They should take on their leadership roles, but they don't." After attending one of this CEO's management meetings, I noticed that she didn't really leave enough space for others to speak up. Intelligent and action-oriented, she knew how to lead a discussion, but appeared to have little time to 'waste' hearing everyone's point of view or building a team reflection. Rather than listening, inquiring, and probing more, she had the answer. She wasn't comfortable letting shared leadership develop to produce real, collective ownership of the decisions being taken.

Leadership, inevitably, is an act of a reciprocal dialogue; the Greek origin of the word '*dia-logos*' actually translates to 'moving forward with words.' Team members who nod in response to the manager's ideas but don't really believe in them isn't a sign of collective intelligence and leadership.

The law of silence stifles creativity and sows the seeds of errors or abuses. Fostering open dialogue, on the other hand, allows a group's intelligence to develop and progress.

The group organization movement means the substitution of intention for accident, of organized purpose for scattered desire. It rests on the solid assumption that this is a man-made not a machine-made world, that men and women are capable of constructing their own life, and that not upon socialism or any rule or any order or any plan or any utopia can we rest our hearts, but only on the force of a united and creative citizenship.

– Mary Parker Follett

Group organization will create the new world we are now blindly feeling after, for creative force comes from the group, creative power is evolved through the activity of the group life.

– Mary Parker Follett

Democratic Leadership versus Guruship

Although leadership entails the notion of guiding people towards a common goal, democratic leaders lead groups by freeing and empowering people to achieve something they commonly desire; whereas authoritarian leaders lead groups by nurturing dependency upon themselves.

With all due respect to the wise gurus of eastern traditions, I make the difference here between *leadership* and what I term *'guruship.'* I refer to 'guruship' here as it's been used in the West to describe the abuse of power of so-called leaders over followers for their own personal interest; a mix of authoritarian and narcissistic dominance, too often misinterpreted as leadership by followers conditioned into a state of dependency.

By commanding, I make you will my will; by guruship, I make you believe that your will is to serve my will and by democratic leadership, I creatively integrate my will with your will into our will. Once you lay out the differences between guruship and leadership, it's easier to understand them.

Table 14 highlights nine of those differences.

Table 14: Differences between guruship and democratic leadership

DIFFERENCES BETWEEN **GURUSHIP** AND **DEMOCRATIC LEADERSHIP**

Guruship	Democratic Leadership
Seeks power "over" people	Seeks power "with" people
Requires blind obedience and personal loyalty	Develops and values the diversity of talents and ideas inorder to better serve the common goal
Affirms to hold "THE "truth	Leaders believe that the interpretation of the truth is much more accurate when every point of view weighs in
Maintains closed, sect-like communities in power-struggles/conflicts with other communities to justify power-over domination by the leader	Creates open and creative communities in dynamic collaboration with other communities, contributing to everyone's development and evolution
Requires the followership's loyalty and service to their person	Maintains loyalty and service to the common purpose
Tries to control through punishment and reward	Leads and steers with shared purpose and common values as a community
Engenders fear, in-fighting, and collective distrust	Engenders trust, cooperation and innovation
Creates dependency on the leader	Creates flourishing communities of leaders
Creates dynamics of idolatry that disempower	Creates dynamics of shared leadership that empower

Appreciative Leading is Inclusive of Diversity

Surviving on a desert island, baking the best cake, or becoming the next top model... all of these emotionally charged reality shows are based on competition, but even more so on the human need for social inclusion and its conjunctive fear of exclusion. The fear of being judged, eliminated, not being good enough... This captivates audiences as vicarious fixes of emotionally charged fears being played-out. Leadership, on the other hand, is inclusive of diversity, it creates safe environments which are open and appreciative of different ideas and different people.

Appreciative leadership builds unity, engagement, innovation, and ethics, less by fear and control and more by inclusiveness and a sense of community, a sense of 'oneness'. By creating safe and inclusive environments, groups also create more authentic cultures and therefore more integrity within the system.

As Srivastva, Fry and Cooperrider wrote in their seminal work *Appreciative Management and Leadership*:

> The more the group or organization can accept an uncommon voice and promote the voicing of dissent, the greater the executive integrity of the system... When members actively promote diverse expressions, the group becomes more resilient. When members can appreciate one another's diversity, they further the integrity of the system.

Similarly, Kim Cameron's recent research (2017) on positive leadership practices and positive energy in corporations is another eloquent example that shows the direct effect of positive leadership on increased revenues and greater engagement among employees. Cameron's research also shows that performing organizations have three times more energizing networks (i.e. positive relationships within the organization) than low-performing organizations. These latest findings in psychology demonstrate how leaders can be positive energizers; and humans flourish in positive energy. In the same vein, Ignacio Pavez of Case Western Reserve University shows in his award-winning research how appreciative practices are positively linked to group potency and collective self-efficacy (i.e. the collective confidence a group has that it can achieve a task or an objective together). Pavez (2017) found that high-performing teams shared more positive remarks and more authentic positive remarks with each other than lower-performing teams.

What 20 years ago was considered by some as touchy-feely management practices is now clearly becoming powerful positive social science. To read more on-line resources on positive psychology, visit:

- https://www.ippanetwork.org

And for more on appreciative inquiry:

- https://appreciativeinquiry.champlain.edu

While negative affectivity is notably linked to the phenomenon of learned helplessness, positive affect is intimately connected with social helpfulness. Somehow positive affect draws us out of ourselves, pulls us away from self-oriented preoccupation, enlarges our focus on the potential good in the world, increases feelings of solidarity with others, and propels us to act in more altruistic and prosocial ways.

– David Cooperrider

Sympathy, born of our union, rises above both egoism and altruism. Sympathy is sense of community, consciousness of oneness.

— Mary Parker Follett

There is no greater power than a community discovering what it cares about.

– Margaret Wheatley

Now, what does all of this mean in this great period of history? It means that we've got to stay together. We've got to stay together and maintain unity. You know, whenever Pharaoh wanted to prolong the period of slavery in Egypt, he had a favorite, favorite formula for doing it. What was that? He kept the slaves fighting among themselves. But whenever the slaves get together, something happens in Pharaoh's court, and he cannot hold the slaves in slavery. When the slaves get together, that's the beginning of getting out of slavery. Now let us maintain unity.

– Martin Luther King Jr.

Consulting Anecdote from the Field
Appreciating as a Collective:
Ken and the Law of the Situation

When I participate in the Significant Leader Exercise, my own example of a significant leader is one of those imprint moments of good appreciative leadership in my career: his name is Ken Wollack.

Ken was (and still is) president of the National Democratic Institute for International Affairs (NDI) in Washington DC. And Ken was my boss during my tenure in the mid-1990s as their field representative in Burundi, Africa, a war-torn and fledgling new democracy.

The quality that struck me most about Ken as my #1 example of leadership was his ability to listen, and to find solutions to very difficult and complex situations by just good listening.

One time in particular, his capacity to listen to the facts and examine with us the situation helped reveal the path forward at a crisis point of our two-year mission in Burundi.

Here is a memorable moment from those times which exemplifies well Ken's outstanding appreciative leadership: The board of directors of NDI met in Washington D.C. one April morning in 1996, and the front page of that day's *Washington Post* had a gruesome picture captioned 'Massacre in Burundi.' Shocked by the news, the board's reaction was explosive: *What are we still doing there? Let's get our guys out right now!* The response was unanimous and unequivocal. Our president telephoned us that evening, telling us the news of the board's decision: it was time to pack our bags.

My colleague and old friend Jean Lavoie and I were dumbfounded. Despite these most recent attacks taking place in specific war-torn slums, we felt leaving Burundi at this particular moment would be the worst of all decisions. We were a few months away from completing an educational tool in both Kirundi and French, serving educational efforts for years. Suddenly leaving as a response to these recent attacks would only reward the divisionists (on both sides) and their tactics to scare away proponents of democracy and unification. Jean and I, each in our turn, tried to convince Ken to review the board's decision demanding our immediate departure. We asked Ken to go back to the board (his bosses), to trust our judgment on the ground, and to reassess their rapid decision so we could complete our mandate.

The American ambassador to Burundi Robert Krueger, one of the most courageous men I have ever met, intervened on our behalf. Ken flew us back to Washington, D.C., to reevaluate our presence in the country. Ken could have very well said, 'OK guys. Good work. Now come back home. Period.' But Ken listened.

And what impressed me most for the rest of my career was *the way he listened* once we met to reevaluate our Burundi mission back in his office in DC.

Once in Ken's office, eight people involved in the East Africa program, including me, sat in a big circle around Ken's desk. All of us were there to discuss whether we should continue our efforts to support the fragile democratic institutions or to leave because of the rising insecurity. It was a complex situation, and we were all very aware that Ken had the last word.

He opened the meeting and asked that we all share our opinions on the situation. To my surprise, he remained very quiet and just listened. He spoke few words, mostly to question and probe. I was surprised at how much freedom he gave us to express ourselves. But I was especially surprised at the way the meeting evolved. One by one, we shared our opinions and perspectives, he asked questions, and after listening to us for nearly an hour, he recapitulated in a few words the essence of what we'd been saying. He then proposed we return to Burundi to complete our mandate, appropriately, while developing an exit strategy. There was a silence of approval in the room. After too many roller-coaster discussions on this question, Ken had just summarized *the* best strategy in a few sentences, which brought us all together in an instant. After so much debate over this issue, I was impressed to see how a leader could, simply by good listening, lead us to find the perfect solution to a very complex situation. Ken didn't have the last word by imposing it; he successfully decoded what Mary Parker Follett called the *law of the situation* with us: he mirrored it back to us, and the last word was actually the situation's last word, which Ken, as a great leader, had helped us decipher and re-unify us around it to move forward.

The democratic leader is not necessarily the one 'who knows' but the one who knows how to bring people to a *collective knowing*, a *collective feeling*, and *a collective willing*.

Ken exemplified what Follett—a century ago—called in decision-making terms, "obeying the law of the situation," another excellent example of scientific management and leadership as an integrative process.

...My solution is to depersonalize the giving of orders, to unite all concerned in a study of the situation, to discover the law of the situation and obey that. ...One person should not give orders to another person, but both should agree to take orders from the situation... From one point of view, one might call the essence of scientific management the attempt to find the law of the situation.

– Mary Parker Follett

Intelligence shifts from being the capacity to solve a problem to the capacity to enter into a shared world of significance.

– Varela, Thompson, and Rosch

Creating Collective Leadership by Creating Times
to Appreciate Together

Some managers are good at avoiding group discussions and are more comfortable managing issues on a one-on-one basis. And then you often hear them say, "But I told my staff what to do; how did they lose track?"

The question is whether we create time and space to appreciate and make sense together, so that groups truly integrate shared intentions. Appreciating together to really listen to everyone's perspective on a situation without falling into collective reactivity and hyperactivity to fix the situation. Appreciating together by welcoming the new employee and making her feel included and us better with her. Appreciating together when at the end of the first sharing of perspective something new and better emerges.

Here are a few examples of ways in which organizations have structured their own appreciative times to reconnect, learn, and celebrate.

Google's TGIF and Q&A Meetings

As a way to lead its exponential growth, Google designed weekly meetings they called TGIF (Thank Goodness it's Friday) as well as Q&A meetings. TGIF is a meeting for executives to reflect on the past week and to see what new ideas have emerged.

The Q&A meetings are opportunities for employees to ask top executives any question in a simple and collegial format. Good examples of making time to appreciate and learn.

Rituals of Individual and Collective Recognition

As the saying goes, 'celebrating success engenders success!' Whether it's a weekly meeting or an opportunity to celebrate a key achievement, leading organizations create their own unique rituals to appreciate, include, value, and build community.

Invent your own rituals, and make sure your recognition is authentic. Phony praise backfires. Good recognition is authentic, concrete, and specific.

Training Programs as 'Strategic Intelligence Cells'

I've found throughout my consulting career that leadership trainings are great for leadership development but they're also what I call 'strategic intelligence cells.'. The degree to which small groups shared beyond the essential content, and, consequently, created a learning process within the organization.

Whatever the training you organize, remember that every group can become a self-reflective and learning community within the system. You have a training on x topic? Why not take the opportunity to add a few additional questions?

Wilfred Bion's
'The Good Group Spirit'

I'd like to share with you an excerpt from British psychiatrist Wilfred Bion's seminal book *Experiences in Groups* from 1957. Bion presents key characteristics of what he terms "the good group spirit."

I've studied and worked in this field of organizational psychology for more than 20 years, and I find that this Bion one-pager, on the next page, still gives us the basics on group dynamics and in a very concise way. I give it to my clients; you could photocopy the page and distribute it around the office as professional and personal development material.

As we become more intelligent in groups, Bion's criteria for a "good group spirit" guide us wisely.

The bold emphasis is mine.

"The Good Group Spirit"

"We are now in a better position to define the 'good group spirit' that has been our aim. It is as hard to define as is the concept of good health in an individual; but some of its qualities appear to be associated with:

*a) **A common purpose**, whether that be overcoming an enemy or defending and fostering an ideal or a creative construction in the field of social relationships or in physical amenities.*

*b) **Common recognition** by members of the group **of the 'boundaries' of the group** and their position and function in relation to those larger units or groups.*

*c) The capacity to absorb new members, and to lose members without fear of losing group individuality – i.e. **'group character'** must be flexible.*

*d) **Freedom from internal sub-groups having rigid (i.e. exclusive) boundaries.** If a sub-group is present it must not be centred on any of its members nor on itself-treating other members of the main group as if they did not belong within the main group barrier—and the **value of the sub-group to the function of the main group must be generally recognized.***

*e) **Each individual member is valued for his contribution to the group** and has free movement within it, his freedom of locomotion being limited only by the generally accepted conditions devised and imposed by the group.*

*f) **The group must have the capacity to face discontent** within the group and must have means to cope with discontent.*

*g) **The minimum size of the group is three.** Two members have personal relationships; with three or more there is a change of quality (interpersonal relationship)."*

- Wilfred Bion (1957)

Leading Intentionally as a Collective

What we will together

Collective leadership is about acting with voluntary shared intent. And in a free and creative world, leadership is about leading a group to its own collective will. A collective will which then becomes its driving and cohesive group force.

Its *Invisible Leader*.

The deeper truth, perhaps the deepest, is that "the will to will the common will" is the core, the germinating centre of that larger, still larger, ever larger life which we are coming to call the true democracy.

– Mary Parker Follett

Leadership and Shared Willing

If leadership is the capacity to guide forward, a couple or a group will have leadership if all members guide forward, together, with that shared intent. The guiding factor then becomes the shared vision or collective intention of what free individuals want to achieve together, rather than just that of the individual leader. Leading is volitional. Managing change and transformation in organizations can't be achieved through the decisions of super-CEOs or small groups of elites alone, but rather by creating a shared leadership culture, where the parking attendant and the CEO both become part of the same learning and developing community.

Franco Dragone, former Cirque du Soleil and Celine Dion's artistic creator, states: "What's most important in any creative project is the meaning we share together. My ultimate guide in any project is our quest for meaning. 'What do we want to do?'" The leader is responsible for putting into place this shared intent and remaining its ultimate guardian. Otherwise, the risk is to suffer from what Dragone calls "disorientation syndrome," a phenomenon he describes as the gradual loss of focus, in the midst of multiple tasks and emergencies, of the original meaning and intent of a particular course of action.

Leadership involves coming back to the original intent:

What do we really want to do with this project? What is the core intention?

Leader and Leadership

The role of leader has generally been associated with the ability to give vision and direction to others. Although this role remains an important one, leadership becomes more than just transmitting the vision. It involves bringing people's ideas together to create a shared vision that everyone can call their own.

Criticizing the personality cult in leadership literature, professor Henry Mintzberg of McGill University speaks of the value of 'communityship.' We have to find a better balance, as he says, "between the place taken by the leader and the recognition of collective processes as sources of vitality for organizations and our societies." Leadership in this context is more a collective dynamic than an individual achievement.

Dr. Yves Lamontagne, former president of the Quebec Board of Physicians, explained in an interview the importance of leadership as a collaborative act: "In the past, we trained our physicians to be the best in their field. That's okay, but what we really need today is not so much for people to be the best but to be better together."

We're in an increasingly interactive world, where a manager's legitimacy no longer rests on possessing information but in the capacity to create shared meaning out of it, so that free and intelligent people will want to work together. The French management thought leader Hervé Sérieyx speaks of the necessity to develop what he calls 'multiplying management,' a management that "multiplies interactive intelligences around shared objectives."

The greatest challenge for organizations today, therefore, isn't so much leading people as *followers* but rather leading them into being better *collaborators* and *leaders* themselves.

Leadership and Collaborative Processes

Many factors lead us to see leadership today more as a collaborative act:

1. The complexity and interdependency of today's environment makes us collaborate more and more with people from different fields, organizations or cultures to deliver, together, better products or services.

2. The continuous increase in the quantity of information to manage, combined with a greater specialization of fields, also makes it impossible for any single person to know or control all the necessary information. We tend to work in less hierarchical project teams, committees, and networks where collaboration is essential.

3. A better educated workforce expects a work environment where they can participate in decision-making. According to Estelle Morin, professor at HEC Montréal, one of the four key factors that contributes to psychological health at work is that people can "participate in the decisions that

concern them, that they do not feel as mere transmission belts, but feel they can influence the decisions with which they will have to work."

4. The increasing legitimacy of certain feminine values or heart-centered attitudes at work also influences the emergence of a more relational and collaborative view of leadership and power. Qualities such as listening, recognition, and empathy have only recently become legitimized as key characteristics of leadership today.

The Leadership Question: 'What do We Will Together?'

Have you defined your collective intention? Your common purpose? Your invisible leader? Your 'what do we will together'?

Without this shared objective, conditions are set for the usual power games of personal interests, or chronic hyperactivity, which excuses us from authentic dialogue and really defining shared intentions.

If a couple or a group had only one question to ask itself in order to strengthen its leadership, it would be: *'What do we want to do together?'*

Sounds too simple? Try it!

Many writers are laying stress on the 'possibilities' of the collective will; what I wish to emphasize is the necessity of 'creating' the collective will. Many people talk as if the collective will was lying round loose to be caught up whenever we like, but the fact is that we must go to our group and see that it is brought into existence.

—Mary P. Follett

Leadership, Hope and Health

> If you want to build a ship, do not gather your men and women to give them orders, to explain each detail, to tell them where to find things... If you want to build a ship, bring alive in the hearts of your men and women the yearning of the sea.
>
> – Antoine de Saint-Exupéry

Leadership means guiding forward and implies an element of hope in the proposed direction. We elect political leaders to guide us towards a better future. We choose leaders in organizations in the hope that they will lead their projects and teams towards greener pastures. Hope is intrinsic to leadership.

Leaders inspire others in believing they can accomplish something greater together than they would alone. Look at a group of children playing, when one of them shouts, 'Hey, let's play this game!' and all of them rally with the shared expectation that the game will be fun. The question is, do we have the capacity to see our future as hopeful?

In *Resonant Leadership*, Boyatzis and McKee (2002) present hope as a key element of leadership. Integrating research on emotional intelligence at work, they show that a positive emotion, such as hope, has significant effect on:

- Psychological and physical wellbeing

- Reasoning and problem-solving capabilities

- Adaptability to circumstances and people

They also write that negative emotions such as hatred, envy, or resentment generate opposite health effects such as anxiety, stress, and depressive feelings. Thus, building a team or organizational project that inspires hope is not only good for performance, but also good for health.

Hopeful imagery, embedded in discourse, attracts energy and mobilizes intention and action. Positive conversations lead to positive actions.

– Barret & Fry

Leading with shared intentions not only develops an organization's vitality and creativity, but can also prevent much unnecessary distress from lack of direction and shared meaning. Numerous approaches try to facilitate the emergence of shared leadership within organizational change processes. Appreciative Inquiry, an innovative approach developed at Case Western Reserve University in Cleveland, has successfully applied positive psychology principles to develop a strength-based approach to organizational development. According to AI pioneers Frank Barrett and Ronald Fry:

> The capacity to cooperate is more likely to develop by building on strengths rather than working on problems. There is little capacity for creativity and innovation when one is overly concerned with avoiding mistakes or repairing something.
>
> – Barret & Fry

Other approaches such as Open Space Technology, Search Conferences, Theory U, and World Café for example also propose participative methodologies where members of groups can become part of its strategy. Whether it is through sophisticated processes or simply by organizing a good strategy meeting, the intention is to find means by which team members can define and be guided by common values and common ambitions.

Leader and followers are both following the invisible leader the common purpose. The best executives put this common purpose clearly before their group.

– Mary Parker Follett

The purpose of all organization is unity of action.

The root of all unity of action is unity of purpose, singleness of motive.

– Lyndall Urwick

Consulting Anecdotes from the Field

Applying the Yin and Yang Model
to Create Collective Leadership:
The Group Leadership Seminar
Methodology

Inspired by the appreciative inquiry (AI) methodology of organizational change, I developed a collective leadership methodology based on comparable AI principles (i.e., positive and anticipatory), with the appreciative and intentional principles and their respective complementary methodologies: the **Appreciative Assessment** and the **Wall of Intentions**.

I've been using this framework in organizational development workshops with groups of various sizes (i.e., 5-300 participants) with much success since 2008. Whatever the number of people or the length of the group workshop, the Group Leadership Seminar focuses on these two principles and two-step methodologies of the Appreciative Assessment and then the Wall of Intentions.

Both methodologies have proven to be impressively efficient and effective in a wide variety of strategic team-building workshops. And it's also very easy to apply on your own in any group or couple.

(See examples of 10 of these Group Leadership Seminars in Appendix B.)

The Appreciative Assessment Methodology: Appraising, Valuing, and Making Meaning Together

As part of the **Appreciative Assessment**, I invite groups during my workshops to assess their topic of interest (for example, the CEO's proposed new vision, or the CEOs co-defining a vision with everyone in the room) from an appreciative perspective.

I ask them to first identify what they appreciate most about the topic and then identify with them the common factors they value together. By appreciating a particular topic together, a group gains more awareness, makes sense of situations, generates positive energy, relatedness and belonging, and highlights common values and priorities.

The results from the appreciative assessment lead back to a common sense of direction that can later be built upon in the subsequent volitional group exercise, the Wall of Intentions.

The Wall of Intentions Methodology: Willing Together

The **Wall of Intention**s is a participative methodology I designed in 2005 with Mr. Robert Garon, a healthcare executive and former client. The exercise helps to co-define shared intentions through a very simple and efficient participative methodology. I've used this methodology with executive teams of five members to assemblies of 300 managers defining together a common sales strategy in three hours!

I remain continuously impressed by the efficiency of the Group Leadership Seminar as a methodology, by creating cohesion and direction with the appreciative assessment and then generating common intentions and collective ownership quickly with the wall of intentions.

The Wall of Intentions: The Process

After having completed the Appreciative Assessment and cocreated a shared understanding and appreciation of the particular topic and what the group values the most, each participant is invited to imagine that situation or topic one year from the present moment and envision it as accomplished and resolved.

Then, one-by-one, each person is asked to come to the Wall of Intentions and write their #1 intention or priority, in relation to the group or desired situation, that they'd like to make happen one year from now. On the Wall, they complete the sentence: *"I want us as a group to…"*

That process is repeated in a democratic fashion, on a flipchart or a white board, depending on the number of people present. Every person (or, if the group is larger, one representative for each table), in turn, goes up to the Wall of Intentions in front of everyone and writes down the main intention they want to express in one or two words. Each person briefly explains his or her point and hands over the marker to the next person. Every person, one by one, is heard and writes on the board.

This is a powerful exercise by its inclusiveness and emergence. After the first person has written their intention and explained it to the group, subsequent people who come up can write their own intentions for the group or can put an asterisk next to any intention that is already up on the board. Inevitably, visual clusters of intentions emerge.

After the last person has written on the wall, the group can all witness together the clusters of shared intentions that have emerged. These shared intentions can then be used as the group's *invisible leader* (as Mary Parker Follett would say) as *their common purpose, their common will*.

These shared intentions can then be translated into action plans that guide the group to the next milepost.

Figure 7: The Appreciative Assessment

1. What do I appreciate most about (…) that I would certainly not want to lose?

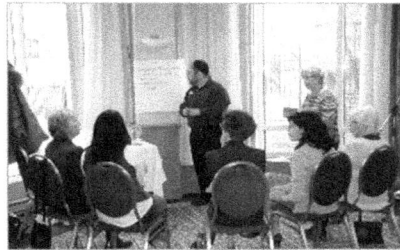

2. Next, identify the themes you all have most in common.

_____

_____

_____

_____

_____

Figure 8: The Wall of Intentions, a powerful and efficient methodology to generate collective willing

Consulting Anecdotes from the Field
10 Group Leadership Seminar Examples

The organizations that hire me for Group Leadership Seminars have generally two objectives in mind: they want to develop the cohesion of their group and they want to move toward a more concrete implementation of a group vision and strategy for the future.

On the next page are 10 examples where I (or people I've coached) applied the Group Leadership Seminar and more specifically *The Appreciative Assessment* and *The Wall of Intentions*.

This two-principled framework has been used for workshops of 90 minutes, half-days, full-days or off-site retreats of multiple days, for executive teams of 5 people up to assemblies of managers and delegates of 300. The great advantage of this leadership model is its adaptability to many contexts and its impressive effectiveness and efficiency in bringing groups together around common values and common ambitions. It's simple to apply and generates results fast because it's grounded in two key generative leadership principles.

View 10 examples of my consulting practice in Table 15 below that I hope will inspire you to apply these principles yourself.

Table 15: Group Leadership Seminar examples*
*For a more detailed description and feedback, see Appendix B.

1. A primary school that had been paralyzed by a longstanding culture of union-management conflict for the last 10 years resurrects and finds new hope in 30 days thanks to the Group Leadership Seminar (2008).

2. Two merging teams of pharmacists of a regional hospital come together for a new beginning together in 2 hours (2016).

3. Coaching of the CEO of a newly created Regional Public Health Agency via telephone in leading a Group Leadership Seminar with her new management team (2015).

4. A cooperative of 120 meat producers redefine a common strategy in 2.5 hours (2012).

5. A newly elected president of a professional order with 70,000 members and 250 permanent staff creates collective leadership for a new era by managing the culture change with Group Leadership Seminars for the whole staff of 250 (2012).

6. A management team of 7 experiences The Group Leadership Seminar in 2 hours and subsequently re-applies the model twice with its entire staff of 100 (2013).

7. 250 account managers of a financial cooperative reflect and commit together to a common sales strategy in 3 hours (2013).

8. 250 members of a professional association redefine a common vision, values and future priorities in 90 minutes, enthusiastically (2015).

9. Seminar by a colleague and part-time rugby coach in a rugby team-building session (2012).

10. Three consecutive annual offsite retreats for a university medical school faculty management team and using the Group Leadership Seminar as framework.

Now, when you sit down to organize your next holidays with your family or friends, why not try the *Appreciative Assessment* and the *Wall of Intentions* to develop your own collective leadership together.

Here's how:

First, the Appreciative Assessment: Ask everyone to identify the top three things they appreciate most of holidays, or that they have most appreciated of your holidays together in the past, and that they value the most. Put everyone's top 3 answers up on the wall and then identify the common themes.

Those are your shared values.

Next, the Wall of Intentions: After you've identified the common themes (values) in the appreciative assessment, create your own Wall of Intentions. Ask everyone to go up to the Wall of Intentions, one-by-one (this is an inclusive exercise where the process requires every single voice for the alchemy to work).

Every person must write down what they'd most want to experience for those holidays to be a success. One-by-one, write your intention for the group or put an asterisk if the intention was already mentioned. Then identify those clusters of shared intentions that can then become the guiding organizing force for your holiday. Those things you will together. And if any unforeseen event questions your direction, come back to your group's original intention! What do we want from this holiday? Have fun!

CONCLUSION

TOWARDS DEMOCRATIC LEADING: EVOLVING FROM DOMINATING TO INTEGRATING

The democratic understanding of leadership as a free and self-directed unifying process, both individually and collectively, parts form the authoritarian understanding of leadership as the ability to command power and control 'over' people and situations.

Democratic leadership, as earlier proposed by democratic philosophers, speaks of leadership as the human capacity to freely cocreate greater unified power 'with' people and situations.

Although the challenges to integration, and leading with democratic values as equals are numerous, the Yin and Yang Model of Leadership helps individuals and collectives from all walks of life in developing and enjoying their own capacity to lead. Whether you are CEO of World Inc., or CEO of your own existence… Or a Burundian military driving a '*Je m'en fous*' truck …!

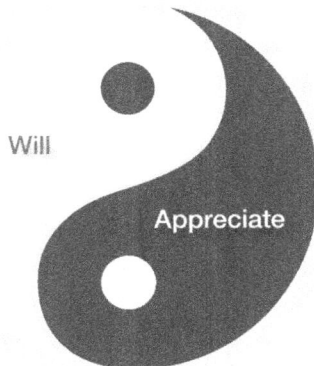

Will

Appreciate

EPILOGUE

As this book is being printed, the Ph.D. version and underlying research conducted with the University of Twente is also near completion. Stay tuned for the upcoming publication of the Ph.D. research for more detailed information on both intentional and appreciative leadership and the relevance of the model for individual and collective leadership development.

APPENDIX A
CORPORATE QUANTITATIVE
EVALUATIONS

Corporate-led quantitative evaluations from 620 of 693 participants from various industries:

Tables 16 to 19 present four sets of client-led quantitative evaluations from 620 participants (i.e., 90 IT Vice-Presidents, 500 IT Managers, 18 Head Oncology nurses and 12 CEOs) who participated in 38 distinct individual leadership workshops using the Yin and Yang Model of Leadership as the underlying framework.

All four sets of quantitative evaluations showed a very high satisfaction rating from all participants. These evaluations weren't designed for the purpose of this book, but they demonstrate the effectiveness and accessibility of the Yin and Yang Model of Leadership for individual and group leadership development workshops.

Table 16: Quantitative Evaluations of individual Leadership workshop from 90 Corporate Vice-Presidents of a global IT company

Very satisfied (4)	Satisfied (3)	Somewhat satisfied (2)	Not satisfied (1)	Average
1. The session topics were relevant and valuable to prepare me for my current role.				
79	11	0	0	3.88/4
2. As a result of this session, I in a better position to understand the value of leadership in my workplace.				
65	24	1	0	3.71/4
3. As a result of this session, I have a better understanding of leadership and the challenges it implies.				
53	35	1	0	3.58/4
4. The skills I gained from this experience can be directly applied to my work.				
78	18	1	0	3.78/4
5. I will be able to use these new skills as soon as I return to work.				
65	25	0	0	3.72/4
6. Overall, the Leadership session satisfied my needs.				
76	14	0	0	3.84/4

YES	NO	N/A
7. Did the session meet your expectations?		
90	**0**	**0**
8. Would you recommend this session to others?		
90	**0**	**0**

Table 17: Quantitative Evaluations of Individual Leadership workshop by 500 managers of a global IT company

Very Satisfied (4)	Satisfied (3)	Somewhat Satisfied (2)	Not Satisfied (1)	Average
1. Overall, the Leadership session satisfied my needs.				
379	109	12	0	3.73/4

YES	NO	N/A
2. Did the session meet your expectations?		
500	**0**	**0**
3. Would you recommend this session to others?		
500	**0**	**0**

Table 18: Quantitative Evaluations of individual Leadership workshop by 18 of the 25 (72%) oncology nurses using the Yin and Yang model as a framework for their workshop

The program was pertinent to my practice	**4.83/5**
The program achieved its set objectives	**4.83/5**
The program fulfilled my learning objective	**4.83/5**
The program was well organized	**5/5**
The length of the program was adequate	**5/5**

Table 19: Quantitative Evaluations of the Individual Leadership Workshop using the Yin and Yang Model as framework from 12 CEOs in Paris

Overall satisfaction	**4.5/5**
Content quality	**4/5**
Clarity of the message	**4.5/5**
Capacity to transmit	**4.5/5**

Appendix B

Detailed Description of 10 Group Leadership Seminar Interventions

PRIMARY SCHOOL

Description

A primary school which had been paralyzed by a longstanding culture of union-management conflict for the last 10 years resurrects and finds new hope in 30 days thanks to the Group Leadership Seminar (2008).

Workshop

Step 1: Proposal to teachers

Propose the Group Leadership Seminar methodology to help the 60 teachers move beyond their toxic culture of conflict and fear.

Step 2: Five 2-hour mini group leadership seminars with subgroups of 12, answering two questions:
1. What they valued most about the school which they would not want to lose
2. In one year from then, what would they most want their school environment to be? One intention.

I gathered the responses to the two questions for each of the five sub-groups and presented the summary results with the whole staff for a 2-hour meeting.

Another 2-hour meeting presentation of the summary results from the 5 sub-groups.

The transformative impact of the intervention began already in step 2 as the subgroups identified what they valued most about their school- and experienced the power of the appreciation.

This longstanding climate was resolved with 30 days and the school embarked on a new and positive future. The feedback below from the former school director which she shared to me 8 years after the actual intervention shows even more how positively transformative the methodology can be. Even in a very conflictual situation.

Feedback

While the school had historically been labeled a "problem school", 7 years after The Group Leadership Seminar intervention the school has now become a model school and referenced as an example for other schools with climate issues. I now refer my friends' children to the school whereas I would have never done so before. Pride is back!

And how this very participative intervention actually emboldened her own leadership as school director. She also writes:

"It has helped my own credibility and legitimacy as a leader to lead such a constructive process through a difficult period."

– Former school director

TWO MERGING PHARMACY DEPARTMENTS

Two merging teams of pharmacists of regional hospital come together for a new beginning together in 2 hours (2016).

Workshop

After a brief introduction, this evening event with the two regional teams newly merging began with an Appreciative Assessment with the following question:

What do I appreciate most about my pharmacy work, which brings me the most satisfaction and that I would not want to lose in this new integrated management?

Then we identified the common themes which actually brought everyone together. And then we completed with the wall of intentions and what they wanted the most to be one year from now; which generated common intentions very quickly and within a positive and constructive spirit.

Here are some of comments from the Director of pharmacy who hired me to facilitate the meeting.

Feedback

"The Seminar allowed us to vent and focus constructively towards the future. The Wall of Intentions really helped our group project itself in the future while allowing everyone to express themselves in a constructive way and all this very quickly."

– Director of pharmacy
merging two regional teams

The aftermath of our 9 December evening has been very energizing and my pharmacists still talk about our Seminar.... we're planning to organize a cocktail soon. At our last management meeting 2 weeks ago, we set priorities until June and we did this with the flip chart sheets the staff filled-out that evening ... to remember what's important to the team ...

– Director of pharmacy

REGIONAL PUBLIC HEALTH AGENCY

Description

Coaching of the CEO of a newly created Regional Public Health Agency via telephone in leading a Group Leadership Seminar with her new management team. (2015)

Workshop

30-minute coaching via telephone of a CEO of a newly created Regional health agency in applying both principles in designing her first management meeting with 16 new directors; all of whom had been her equal in the past and now had to lead a regional health policy together.

She stared her 2-hour Group leadership seminar by asking them to discuss in smaller groups what they valued most of the existing regional health policy and what challenges or aspects they wanted most to improve. After identifying the common elements from the previous two questions, she followed with her own wall of intentions inviting her directors to go one-by-one on the white board and write what they wanted most to become as a regional health agency. The two-hour meeting was a huge success. Her upper cap letters below speak to this efficient success and satisfaction of the CEO.

Feedback

"The Seminar achieved the objective: A shared meaning to give our collective project and constitute a team from talented individuals. The Seminar created COLLECTIVE engagement."

– CEO of a regional public health authority

"In the final roundtable of this 2-hr Group Leadership Seminar we all noticed that we had become a team through this experience and that we knew each other better. We knew 'who had which strength or talent' available to the Team. This thanks to your coaching me how to conduct this exercise with my new management team."

– CEO of regional public health authority

MEAT PRODUCERS

Description

A cooperative of 120 meat producers redefine a common strategy in 2.5 hours (2012).

Workshop

A meat cooperative had 2.5. hours to come to a common vision shared strategies. After a brief introduction, we conducted the Appreciative Assessment and the Wall of Intentions.

As you can see in the executive director's feedback and the quantitative evaluations, the seminar with its appreciative and intentional principles once again showed how efficient they could be in generating collective leadership.

Feedback

"The Group Leadership Seminar was the triggering point which began our whole reflection on the Federation of tomorrow. And our new structure."

– Executive director of a meat cooperative

This *Group Leadership Seminar* program with a corporate evaluation showed that 94% of delegates were either satisfied, very satisfied, or extremely satisfied with their experience of the *Group Leadership Seminar* and the application of the two leadership principles as a strategic exercise. Table 20 displays the results.

**Table 20: Corporate Quantitative Analysis:
Meat-Producing Cooperative**

**Overall Satisfaction of the Group Leadership Seminar
April, 2012**

106 Respondents (n=106)
Response rate = 83.33%

Extremely satisfied	Very satisfied	Satisfied	Dis-satisfied	Very dis-satisfied	Extremely dissatisfied	No comment
25	53	22	1	2	1	2
(23%)	(50%)	(21%)	(1%)	(2%)	(1%)	(2%)

PROFESSIONAL ORDER

Description

A newly elected president of a professional order with 70,000 members and 250 permanent staff creates collective leadership for a new era by managing the culture the Group Leadership Seminars for her whole staff of 250 (2012).

Workshop

The new president of a professional order involved every one of its 250 employees and directors in defining their common future with the Group Leadership through this three-step process:

- 1st step: 1-day group leadership seminar with executive team (5)
- 2nd step: 1-day group leadership seminar with management team (15)
- 3rd step: 2 half-day sessions of group leadership seminar with 50% of the staff in each session (60 x 2)

The direct effects of such an intervention are the efficient building of shared values and shared intentions amidst a positive company-wide cultural change ritual.

Feedback

"It helped us become aware that there were different management philosophies within different departments and the exercise helped us identify more evolved practices which brought us together."

"We're more coherent now. We know what talk we want to walk."

"I found The Wall of Intentions to be a powerful methodology. We often forget to re-focus on collective intentions; a common purpose. And then be able to come back to it. It's a simple way to address questions of values and vision. And the individual way people participate is powerfully engaging."

"A memorable moment for all employees. It's a very powerful and inclusive methodology to create a sense of belonging and cohesion."

"The Seminar allowed us to have more authentic conversations between us."

– Director of nurses' professional order

MANAGEMENT TEAM

Description

A management team of 7 experiences The Group Leadership Seminar in 2 hours and subsequently reapplies the model twice with its entire staff of 100 (2013).

Workshop

I was invited to meet the management team of a financial cooperative branch and lead with them a group leadership seminar and offer training in change management.

After the Appreciative Assessment and Wall of Intentions this group appreciated the exercise so much that it has significantly changed their management practices ever since in a much more appreciative way. It also further legitimized the leader's leadership as it did with the school director in the first example.

Feedback

"I used to address our successes and failures at about the same level. But since the Seminar I now put a deliberate emphasis throughout the organization on the positive."

– Branch Executive Director

"It was a great method to go to the Board with clear and committed priorities adopted throughout the organization."

– Branch Executive Director

"The seminar is an accessible and inclusive methodology for everyone."

– Branch manager

"The experience of this process is a source of accomplishment as a leader."

– Branch Executive Director

FINANCIAL COOPERATIVE

Description

250 account managers of a financial cooperative reflect and commit together to a common sales strategy in 3 hours. (2013)

Workshop

250 financial account managers and directors of a financial cooperative cocreate a common sales strategy at their annual meeting using the two leadership principles in three hours. (2012)

After a brief presentation of the new sales strategy by the senior vice-president and fellow colleagues, all 250 participants were invited to participate in an appreciative assessment of the sales strategy with two questions per table (i.e., 1. What I like the most about the vision?; and, 2. Do I have any concerns?) which generated much enthusiasm and energy. Then followed the Wall of intentions exercise with one representative per table going to the white board on the main stage to write what they would prioritize the most of this vision in the coming year.

At the end of the seminar, the senior vice-president came to me and confided that the four key intentions which his managers had just enthusiastically defined together were exactly the ones he had been trying sell them for years. But this time they were theirs. Leadership was shared.

Feedback

"The Seminar allowed us to have more authentic conversations between us. It brought the Senior Vice-President closer to the managers than ever before. There was a true feeling of all being in it together as we had never spent 3 hours to really reflect together. Especially 250 of us!"

"Mixing everyone together without distinction of title created a sense of belonging and trust. I saw some people open up and share in a positive and constructive way like I would have never imagined."

"Everyone is somewhat 'forced' to participate in the methodology and that is good. Some managers have a tendency to avoid these discussions but this forced them to work through some issues constructively and come out with concrete outputs."

– HR sponsor

PROFESSIONAL ASSOCIATION

Description

Two hundred and fifty (250) members of a professional association enthusiastically redefine a common vision, values and future priorities in 90 minutes (2015).

Workshop

I was originally invited to give a 90-minute conference for this professional IT association and proposed to give them a conference as well as experiment the group leadership seminar themselves.

As you will read below, not only did the association get a conference, but thanks to the seminar they gained a greater sense of identity and belonging around shared values as well as shared intentions for the future.

Feedback

"As to the "appreciative" part I thought this was fantastic. It set up the whole exercise to be positive and successful.
    – IT delegate and executive of IT professional association

"It was refreshing to experience a different way of looking at situations rather than the typical task and problem solving orientation."

"Our Chair, was very pleased that you did the information gathering during the seminar (i.e. Appreciative Assessment and Wall of Intentions), which will be used to make our annual event even better in the coming years!"
    – IT cooperative executive

RUGBY COACH

Description

Seminar by a colleague and part-time rugby coach in a rugby team-building session (2012).

Workshop

A fellow organizational consultant and part-time rugby coach decided to experiment the Group leadership methodology with his rugby team which was going through difficult times. See how the exercise also softened tough hearts and led to a team transformation.

Feedback

"But the craziest was this hard-nose player, who is a typical hard guy from a poor background with a wicked tongue, someone who spoils any forward momentum because he cuts people down, and who has been told he needs to watch how he approaches people for 10 years! He never lets anyone close and never admits warmth or love. But during the final Wall of Intentions exercise he stood up and said to everyone's surprise:

"I was going to say I need to become a better player, but something Colin just said about trust made me see that there is something more important. I need to be more positive, I need to have a better attitude and create a better climate in the club... [Stunned silence.]"

– Rugby team coach

UNIVERSITY MEDICAL SCHOOL

Description

Three consecutive annual offsite retreats for a university medical school faculty management team (2012, 2013, 2014).

Workshop

Each 2-day offsite retreat was designed around the two leadership principles of intentionality and appreciation both for them as leaders and as a team of leaders. This also included each year the Appreciative Assessment and the Wall of Intentions (2012, 2013, 2014).

- 2012: 2-day off-site retreat with executive team. n=12
- 2013: 2-day off-site retreat with executive team. n=12
- 2014: 2-day off-site retreat with executive team. n=12

The Group Leadership Seminar method served as a very positive framework for the team's development but its simplicity actually led the Faculty to integrate it in their own management practices.

Feedback

"It was refreshing to experience a different way of looking at situations rather than the typical task and problem-solving orientation. It's amazing how rapidly the Appreciative Assessment makes you move-up to a different level."
— Executive director of medical faculty

"Our team has matured through these three annual Group Leadership Seminars. We depend less on the Dean to solve every problem and we talk to each other much more."
— Executive director of a medical faculty

"The methodology is accessible and adaptable to any group. We have also integrated the Appreciative Assessment throughout the Faculty as a management practice and we have also self-designed and conducted our own Strategic Planning around this Appreciative-Intentional model with much success."

– Executive Director of medical faculty

"I've used this model many times after the Seminar to solve conflictual situations between people in a very efficient way. I ask them: What do you value about what you do or this situation? And then, What do you want to accomplish in the future? It's powerful and applicable in so many contexts."

– Dean of a medical faculty

"I was impressed by the positive effect of listening and valuing everyone during the workshop on our subsequent relationships at work."

– Medical Faculty Communications Director

"It's a method that makes the participants the authors and leaders rather than having someone telling them what to do."

– Dean of medical faculty

"I have used this model many times after the Seminar to solve conflictual situations between people in a very efficient way. I ask them: What do you value about what you do or this situation? And then, What do you want to accomplish in the future? It's powerful and applicable in so many contexts."

– Dean of medical faculty

ACKNOWLEDGEMENTS

Thank you for your support along the way: Late professors Suresh Srivastva, Don Wolfe, and Retta Holdorf; professors Tojo Thatchenkery, David Kolb, Ronald Fry, David Cooperrider, Bill Pasmor, Richard Boyatzis, Diana Bilamoria, and Susan Case, David Steingard, Gurudev Khalsa, Ann Baker, Pat Rowe, Jay Michela, Marjory Kerr, David Pilon, Jan Bauer and Jean-François Vézina, the more than 2309 leaders who have been contributing to this ongoing research by trusting me with the development of their own leadership and that of their teams and organizations.

André Héon, Lucile Beaubien, Danièle Héon and Elise Héon, Paul Beaubien, Lise Bétournay, Alexandra Beaubien, and Boubou; Etienne Godard and Nathalie Arel, Ivan Drouin, Liliane Auger, Pierre Agard, Jean-Marie Lapointe, Stephen Sims, Eddie Grell, François Leduc, Wendy Schmidt, Stéphanie Rivier, Sébastien Damart, Albie Davis, Jennifer Jones-Patulli and Anne Coyle, Denis Cocquet, and the whole network of innovative leaders at APM.fr, Lucie Dugal, Jean Lavoie and the Lavoie family, Marc Girard, Midori Inoue, Laurent Chartier, Laïla Chraïbi, Herman Wittockx and the Wittockx family, François Lapointe, Marianne Sicari, Angel Margaret Poku and Mary Poku, Sheila McNamee, Celeste Wilderom, Cecile Betit, Lindsey Godwin and William Hancy, Lisa Nelson, Paige Stirling and last and thankfully for this project, Carole Zabbal-Wynne whose generous and professional editing assistance, once again, has made this self-publishing adventure possible, and your reading experience much more enjoyable.

BIBLIOGRAPHY

Akrivou, K. (2008). *Differentiation and integration in adult development: The influence of self-complexity and integrative learning on self-integration* (Doctoral dissertation).

Altmäe, S., Türk, K., & Toomet, O. S. (2013). Thomas-Kilmann's *Conflict Management* Modes and their relationship to Fiedler's Leadership Styles (basing on Estonian organizations). Baltic Journal of Management, 8(1), 45-65.

Asch, S.E. (1955). "Opinions and social pressure," *Scientific American*. 193 (5): 31–35. doi:10.1038/scientificamerican1155-31.

Bakhtin, M. M. (2010). *The dialogic imagination: Four essays* (Vol. 1). Austin, TX: University of Texas Press.

Barbaranelli, C., Caprara, G. V., & Maslach, C. (1997). *Individuation and the five-factor model of personality traits.* European Journal of Psychological Assessment, 13(2), 75-84.

Barrett, F. J. & Fry, R. E. (2008). *Appreciative inquiry: A positive approach to building cooperative capacity.* Chagrin Falls, OH: Taos Institute Publications.

Barrett, F. J. (2012). *Yes to the mess: Surprising leadership lessons from jazz.* Harvard Cambridge, MA: Harvard Business School Publishing.

Bass, B. M. (1985). *Leadership and performance beyond expectations.* New York: Free Press.

Bass, B. M. (1990). *Bass & Stogdill's handbook of leadership: Theory, research, and managerial applications* (3rd ed.). New York: Free Press.

Bass, B. M. (1999). "Two decades of research and development in transformational leadership." *European Journal of Work and Organizational Psychology*, 8, 9–32.

Bass, B. M. & Avolio, B. J. (1997). *Full range leadership development: Manual for the Multifactor Leadership Questionnaire*. Palo Alto, CA: Mind Garden.

Bass, B. M. & Bass, R. (2008). *The Bass handbook of leadership: Theory, research, and managerial applications* (4th ed.). New York: Free Press.

Bauer, J. (1985). "L'individuation. " *Les conférences du Cercle C. G. Jung de Montréal*. Unpublished manuscript.

Bennis, W. (2009). *On becoming a leader*. Basic Books.

Bion, W. R. (2013). *Experiences in groups: and other papers*. Routledge.

Blake, R. & Mouton, J. (1964). *The managerial grid: The key to leadership excellence*. Houston, TX: Gulf Publishing.

Boje, D. M., Gephart, Jr., R. P., & Thatchenkery, T. J. (1996). *Postmodern management and organization theory*. Thousand Oaks, CA: Sage Publications.

Bowden, A. O. (1926). "Study of the personality of student leaders in colleges in the United States." *Journal of Abnormal and Social Psychology*, 21, 149–160.

Boyatzis, R. E. (1998). *Transforming qualitative information: Thematic analysis and code development*. Thousand Oaks, CA: Sage Publications.

Boyatzis, R. E. (1999). "Self-directed change and learning as a necessary meta-competency for success and effectiveness in the twenty-first century," in R. R. Sims & J. G. Veres (Eds.), *Keys to employee success in coming decades* (pp. 15-32). Westport, CT: Quorum Books.

Boyatzis, R. E. (2006). "An overview of intentional change from a complexity Perspective," *Journal of Management Development*, 25(7), 607-623.

Boyatzis, R. E. (2008). "Leadership development from a complexity perspective." *Consulting Psychology Journal: Practice and Research*, 60(4), 298-313.

Boyatzis, R. E. & Kolb, D. A. (1991). "Assessing individuality in learning: The learning skills profile," *Educational Psychology, 11*(3-4), 279-295.

Burke, C. S., Stagl, K. C., Klein, C., Goodwin, G. F., Salas, E., & Halpin, S. M. (2006). "What type of leadership behaviors are functional in teams? A meta-analysis." *The Leadership Quarterly*, 17(3), 288-307.

Burns, J. M. (1978). *Leadership*. New York: Harper Collins.

Bennis, W., & Bennis, W. G. (2010). *On becoming a leader*. ReadHowYouWant.com.

Cameron, K. (2017). Paradox in Positive Organizational Scholarship. *The Oxford Handbook of Organizational Paradox*, 216.

Capra, F. & Flatau, M. (1996). "Emergence and design in human organizations: creative tension 'at the edge of chaos,' *Complexity and Management Paper*s, (9).

Carlyle, T. (1840). *On heroes, hero-worship, and the heroic in history*. Boston: Houghton-Mifflin.

Carson, J. B., Tesluk, P. E., & Marrone, J. A. (2007). "Shared leadership in teams: An investigation of antecedent conditions and performance." *Academy of Management Journal, 50*(5), 1217-1234.

Chan, W. (2008). *A source book in Chinese philosophy*. Princeton University Press.

Collins, J. C. (2001). *Good to great*. New York: Harper Collins.

Collins, J. C. & Porras, J. I. (1994). *Built to last*. New York: Harper Collins.

Contractor, N. S., DeChurch, L. A., Carson, J., Carter, D. R., & Keegan, B. (2012). "The topology of collective leadership," *The Leadership Quarterly*, 23(6), 994-1011.

Corballis, M. C. (1992). *On the evolution of language and generativity. Cognition*. Volume 44, Issue 3, 1992, 197–226.

Daft, R. L. (2008). *The leadership experience.* Mason, Ohio: Thomson/South-Western.

Day, D. V., Gronn, P., & Salas, E. (2006). "Leadership in team-based organizations: On the threshold of a new era," *The Leadership Quarterly,* 17(3), 211-216.

Dansereau, F., Seitz, S. R., Chiu,, C.-Y., Shaughnessy, B., & Yammarino, F. J. (2013). "What makes leadership, leadership? Using self-expansion theory to integrate traditional and contemporary approaches," *The Leadership Quarterly, 24*(6), 798-821.

DeGeus, A. (1997). *The living company: habits for survival in a turbulent environment.* London: Nicholas Brealey.

Dinh, J. E., Lord, R. G., Gardner, W. L., Meuser, J. D., Liden, R. C., & Hu, J. (2014). "Leadership theory and research in the new millennium: Current theoretical trends and changing perspectives," *The Leadership Quarterly, 25*(1), 36-62.

Eberly, M. B., Johnson, M. D., Hernandez, M., & Avolio, B. J. (2013). "An integrative process model of leadership: Examining loci, mechanisms, and event cycles," *American Psychologist,* 68(6), 427-443.

Follett, M. P. (1918). "The new state: Group organization, the solution of popular government." New York: Longmans, Green and Co. New York.

Gardner. J. W. (1989). *On leadership.* New York: Free Press.

Greenleaf, R. K. (2002). *Servant Leadership: A Journey into the Nature of Legitimate Power and Greatness* (25th anniversary ed.). New York: Paulist Press

Fiedler, F. E. (1967). *A Theory of Leadership Effectiveness,* New York: McGraw-Hill.

Frankl, V. E. (1955). *The doctor and the soul. An introduction to logotherapy.* New York: Random House.

Gardner. J. W. (1989). *On leadership.* New York: Free Press.

Gibb, C. A. (1947). "The principles and traits of leadership," *Journal of Abnormal and Social Psychology, 42*, 267-284.

Glaser, B. G. & Strauss, A. L. (1967). *The discovery of grounded theory: Strategies for qualitative research*. Chicago: Aldine Publishing.

Goleman, D., Boyatzis, R., & McKee, A. (2002). *Primal leadership: Realizing the power of emotional intelligence*. Harvard Business School Press, USA.

Graham, P. (1995). *Mary Parker Follett: The prophet of management: a celebration of writings from the 1920s*. Cambridge, MA: Harvard Business Press.

Guzzo, R. A., & Shea, G. P. (1992). "Group performance and intergroup relations in organizations," *Handbook of Industrial and Organizational Psychology*, 3, 269-313.

Hackman, J. R. & Wageman, R. (2007). "Asking the right questions about leadership: Discussion and conclusions," *American Psychologist, 62*(1), 43-47.

Hallowell, E. (2005). "Overloaded Circuits: Why Smart People Underperform." *Harvard Business Review*. January Issue.

Halpin, A. W. (1957). *Manual for the leader behavior description questionnaire*. Columbus, OH: Fisher College of Business, the Ohio State University.

Hartranft, C. (2003). *The Yoga-Sûtra of Patañjali: A new translation with commentary*. Boston: Shambhala.

Hayes, S. C. (2004). "Acceptance and commitment therapy, relational frame theory, and the third wave of behavioral and cognitive therapies," *Behavior Therapy, 35*(4), 639-665.

Heidegger, M. (1962). *Being and time*. 1927. Trans. John Macquarrie and Edward Robinson. New York: Harper.

Hemphill, J. K. & Coons, A. E. (1957). *Leader behavior: Its description and measurement*. Columbus, OH: Ohio State University Bureau of Business Research.

Hersey, P. & Blanchard, K. H. (1969). *Management of organizational behavior*. Englewood Cliffs, NJ: Prentice-Hall.

Hersted, L. & Gergen, K. J. (2013) *Relational leading: Practices for dialogically based collaboration*. Chagrin Falls, OH: Taos Institute Publications.

Hocks, E. D. (1996). "Dialectic and the 'two forces of one power,'" *Tradition and Discovery: The Polanyi Society Periodical*, 23(3), 4-16.

Hollenbeck, J. R., Beersma, B., & Schouten, M. E. (2012). "Beyond team types and taxonomies: A dimensional scaling conceptualization for team description*,*" *Academy of Management Review*, 37(1), 82-106.

Jacquard, A. (2005). *Travailler en réseau dans un monde de plus en plus complexe*. Québec : Esse Leadership.

Jung, C. G. (1923/1971). *Theory of the types: The portable Jung* (H. G. Baynes, Trans.). New York: Penguin Books.

Kahane, A. (2010). *Power and love: A theory and practice of social change*. San Francisco: Berrett-Koehler.

Kolb, D. A. (1984). *Experiential learning: experience as the source of learning and development*. Englewood Cliffs, NJ: Prentice-Hall.

Kolb, D. A. (1988). "Integrity, advanced professional development, and learning," in S. Srivastva, *Executive integrity: The search for high human values in organizational life* (pp. 74-98). New York: Jossey-Bass

Kolb, D. A., Boyatzis, R. E., & Mainemelis, C. (2001). "Experiential learning theory: Previous research and new directions," *Perspectives on Thinking, Learning, and Cognitive Styles*, 1, 227-247.

Korman, A. K. (1966). "Consideration, initiating structure, and organizational criteria: A review," *Personnel Psychology*, (19)4, 349-361.

Kouzes, J. M., & Posner, B. Z. (2006). *The leadership challenge (Vol. 3).* John Wiley & Sons.

LePine, J. A., Piccolo, R. F., Jackson, C. L., Mathieu, J. E., & Saul, J. R. (2008). "A meta-analysis of teamwork processes: tests of a multidimensional model and relationships with team effectiveness criteria," *Personnel Psychology, 61*(2), 273-307.

Ogilvy, J. (2010). "Strategy and intentionality," *World Futures,* 66(2), 73-102.

Maas, P. A. (2013). "A Concise Historiography of Classical Yoga Philosophy," *Historiography and Periodization of Indian Philosophy,* 53-90.

Marks, M. A., Mathieu, J. E., & Zaccaro, S. J. (2001). "A temporally based framework and taxonomy of team processes," *Academy of Management Review, 26*(3), 356-376.

May, R. (1969). *Love and will.* New York: W. W. Norton & Company.

McGregor, D. (1960). *The human side of enterp*rise. New York: McGraw Hill.

Metcalf, H. C. (1926). *Scientific foundations of business administration.* Baltimore: Williams & Wilkins.

Metcalf, H. C. (1927). *Business management as a profession.* Chicago: A. W. Shaw.

Metcalf, H. C. & Urwick, L., Eds. (1941). *The collected papers of Mary Parker Follett.* Bath, UK: Management Publications Trust.

Milgram, Stanley (1963). "Behavioral Study of Obedience," *Journal of Abnormal and Social Psychology.* 67 (4): 371-8. PMID 14049516. doi:10.1037/h0040525 as PDF. Archived 2015-04-04 at the Wayback Machine.

Mintzberg, H. (2008). "Leadership et communityship." *Gestion,* 33(3), 16-17.

Morin, E. (2011). *La Voie: Pour l'avenir de l'humanité.* Fayard.

Öst, L. G. (2008). "Efficacy of the third wave of behavioral therapies: A systematic review and meta-analysis," *Behavior Research and Therapy*, 46(3), 296-321.

Pages, M. (1990). "The illusion and disillusion of appreciative management," *Appreciative Management and Leadership: The Power of Positive Thought and Action in Organizations*, 353-380.

Pavez, I. (2017, January). "A Micro-Level Integration of Diagnostic and Appreciative Approaches: A Paradoxical Approach. In Academy of Management Proceedings," (Vol. 2017, No. 1, p. 10589). *Academy of Management*.

Pearce, C. L. & Conger, J. A. (2002). *Shared leadership: Reframing the hows and whys of leadership*. New York: Sage Publications.

Quinn, R. E., Spreitzer, G. M., & Hart, S. (1992). "Challenging the assumptions of bipolarity: Interpenetration and effectiveness," in S. Srivastva and R. Fry (Eds.), *Executive continuity* (pp. 222-229). San Francisco: Jossey-Bass.

Rosenberg, M. B. (1999). *Nonviolent communication: A language of compassion* . Del Mar, CA: PuddleDancer Press.

Roskies, E., Seraganian, P., Oseasohn, R., Hanley, J. A., Collu, R., Martin, N., & Smilga, C. (1986). "The Montreal Type A Intervention Project: Major findings," *Health Psychology*, 5(1), 45.

Scharmer, C. O. (2009). *Theory U: Learning from the future as it emerges*. Berrett-Koehler Publishers.

Schein, E. H. (1985). *Organizational culture and leadership*. San Francisco: Jossey-Bass.

Schein, E. H. (2013). *Humble inquiry: The gentle art of asking instead of telling*. Oakland, CA: Berrett-Koehler.

Schiller, M., Holland, B. M., & Riley, D. (2002). *Appreciative leaders: In the eye of the beholder*. Chagrin Falls, OH: Taos Institute Publications.

Simonton. A, C. (1997). *The leadership balance. Confessions of a Management Consultant Turned CEO.* Knoxville, TN: SPC Press.

Sivananda, S. (1994). *Devi Mahatmya.* Divine Life Society.

Smith, M. E., Van Oosten, E. B., & Boyatzis, R. E. (2009). "Coaching for sustained desired change," in R. W.Woodman, W. A. Pasmore, & A. B. Shani (Eds.), *Research in organizational change and development* (pp. 145-173), Bingley, UK: Emerald Group Publishing, Ltd.

Smith, W. K., Besharov, M. L., Wessels, A. K., & Chertok, M. (2012). "A paradoxical leadership model for social entrepreneurs: Challenges, leadership skills, and pedagogical tools for managing social and commercial demands," *Academy of Management Learning & Education,* 11(3), 463-478.

Sorenson, G. (2000, August-September). "An intellectual history of leadership studies: The role of James MacGregor Burns," *Annual meeting of the American Political Science Association*, Washington D.C., Retrieved Feb. 5, 2005, from http://www.academy.umd.edu/publications/presidential_leaders hip/sorenso_apsa.htm

Srivastva, S. (1989, March). *Opening address to Executive Integrity Summit*, Case Western Reserve University, March, 21. Unpublished address.

Srivastva, S (Ed.), *Executive integrity: The search for high human values in organizational life* (pp. 15-34). New York: Jossey-Bass.

Srivastva, S. & Barrett, F. J., (1988). "Foundations for executive integrity,," Executive Integrity: The Search for High Human Values in Organizational Life (pp. 290-320). San Francisco: Jossey-Bass.

Srivastva, S. & Cooperrider, D. (1990). *Appreciative management and leadership: The power of positive thought and action in organizations.* San Francisco: Jossey-Bass.

Srivastva, S., Fry, R., & Cooperrider, D. (1989). "A call for executive appreciation," in S. Srivastva, *Executive integrity: The search for high human values in organizational life* (pp. 15-34). New York: Jossey-Bass.

Steingard, D. S., & Dufresne, R. L. (2011). "Intentional intelligence and the intentional intelligence quotient (IIQ): Construct development and scale validation integrating mindfulness, self-agency, and positive thought flow," *Journal of Management, Spirituality & Religion, 8*(1), 3-22.

Stevens, A. (2002). *Archetype revisited: An updated natural history of the self.* Toronto: Inner City Books.

Stogdill, R. M. (1948). "Personal factors associated with leadership: A survey of the literature," *Journal of Psychology, 25,* 35–71. doi:10.1080/00223980.1948.9917362

Stogdill, R. M., & Coons, A. E. (1957). *Leader behavior: Its description and measurement.* Columbus, OH: Ohio State University Press for Bureau of Business Research.

Stout, M. & Love, J. M. (2015) "Integrative Process: Follettian Thinking from Ontology to Administration," *Toward Ecological Civilization* series. Process Century Press.

Tead, O. (1935). *The art of leadership.* Oxford, England: Whittlesey House (McGraw-Hill).

Thatchenkery, T. & Metzker, C. (2006). *Appreciative intelligence: Seeing the mighty oak in the acorn.* San Francisco: Berrett-Koehler.

Taylor C. (1992). *Grandeur et misère de la modernité.* Toronto: Anansi Press.

Thomas, K. W. (1974). *Thomas-Kilmann conflict mode instrument.* Tuxedo, NY: Xicom.

Urwick, L. (1935). "The problem of organization: A study of the work of Mary Parker Follett," *Taylor Bulletin*, 5.

Van Oosten, E. B. (2006). "Intentional change theory at the organizational level: a case study." *Journal of Management Development,* 25(7), 707-717.

Weick, K. E. (1979). "Cognitive processes in organizations," *Research in Organizational Behavior*, *1*(1), 41-74.

Weick, K. E. (1996, October) "The attitude of wisdom: Ambivalence as the optimal compromise." Paper presented at the International Symposium on Organizational Wisdom and Courage, Department of Organizational Behavior, Case Western Reserve University, Cleveland, OH.

Weinberg, G. M. (1975). *An introduction to general systems thinking*.

Weisbord, M. R. (1992). *Discovering common ground*. San Francisco: Berrett-Koehler.

Weissenberg, P. & Kavanagh, M. J. (1972). "The independence of initiating structure and consideration: A review of the evidence," *Personnel Psychology, 25*(1), 119-130.

Whitney, D., Trosten-Bloom, A., & Rader, K. (2010). *Appreciative leadership:* Focus on what works to drive winning performance and build a thriving organization. New York: McGraw-Hill.

Zeitouni, J.-M. (2008*). Jouer son rôle de leader, sans fausse note !* Québec : Magazine Vivre, Sep.-Oct. 2008.

ABOUT FRANÇOIS

François completed his Master's degree in industrial/ organizational psychology at the University of Waterloo in Ontario and then pursued his Ph.D. coursework in organizational behavior at Case Western Reserve University's Weatherhead School of Management in Cleveland.

He then worked on institutional change projects in Romania (1991) and Burundi (1994-1996), and began an ongoing collaboration with Organizational Behavior Development in Belgium conducting international leadership programs.

Back in Canada in 1996, François took on new challenges with the development and management of alternative support services for psychiatric patients in the community. It is in this context that he discovered his talent and passion for individual accompaniment and pursued clinical training at McGill's Allen Memorial Institute.

Yearning to return to the field of consulting with his management and clinical experience, he then took the leadership of Adecco Canada's new consulting division, The House of Leaders (2002-2005) and pursued this last project in its transition to become Esse Leadership (2005-2009).

In 2009, François chose to pursue his passion for the development of leaders and groups by working under his own name, while continuing ongoing partnerships in Canada and internationally.

François has worked with several different types of clients in many industries to develop their leadership potential through workshops and seminars.

He has recently co-edited writings of management pioneer Mary Parker Follett published on Amazon: *Mary Parker Follett: Ideas We Need Today*, translated in French, Arabic and soon in Dutch.

He holds a Ph.D. from the University of Twente (The Netherlands), studying the successful impact on former clients of the Yin and Yang Leadership Model he developed for individuals and collectives.

www.ingramcontent.com/pod-product-compliance
Lightning Source LLC
Chambersburg PA
CBHW071537200326
41519CB00021BB/6513